LEAD LIKE WALT

Discover Walt Disney's Magical Approach to Building Successful Organizations

Pat Williams

with Jim Denney

Foreword by NBA Stars Robin Lopez and Brook Lopez

Health Communications, Inc.
Deerfield Beach, Florida

www.hcibooks.com

W9-AQI-414

Library of Congress Cataloging-in-Publication Data
is available through the Library of Congress

© 2019 Pat Williams

ISBN-13: 978-07573-2196-2 (Paperback)
ISBN-10: 07573-2196-8 (Paperback)
ISBN-13: 978-07573-2199-3 (ePub)
ISBN-10: 07573-2199-2 (ePub)

Publisher: Health Communications, Inc.
         3201 S.W. 15th Street
         Deerfield Beach, FL 33442–8190

Cover and interior design by Lawna Patterson Oldfield

Praise for *Lead Like Walt*

"In *Lead Like Walt*, Pat Williams and Jim Denney have captured the management, leadership, and creative talent Walt Disney possessed. I often use one of Walt's quotes in my seminars: 'Always fight for quality, whether giving or receiving.' During my time as Executive Vice President of Operations for the Walt Disney World® Resort I often thought, like many Cast Members do, *What would Walt do?* If you want to be great at what you do, I suggest you study this book and learn from Walt, and then you will know what to do when opportunities and obstacles appear in your life."

—Lee Cockerell
Executive Vice President (retired and inspired), Walt Disney World® Resort
Author of *Creating Magic: 10 Common Sense Leadership Strategies from a Life At Disney*

"We all know Disney the company, but some may have overlooked Disney the man. Pat Williams and Jim Denney bring Walt Disney to life in *Lead Like Walt*. Disney was part visionary, part entrepreneur, and part creative genius. Walt meshed the parts together through his leadership by bringing people together to share in that vision. Walt used his imagination to conceive of where to go next, but he challenged his team to bring those visions to life. Disney's leadership serves as an example of how to bring great people together in order to create a bigger, bolder, and brighter future. *Lead Like Walt* is a joy to read and, as all books by Pat Williams, it is a rich reservoir of leadership wisdom."

—John Baldoni
Inc.com Top Leadership Expert and Speaker, Executive Coach
Bestselling Author of 14 Books, Including *GRACE: A Leader's Guide to a Better Us*

"Pat Williams has done a remarkable job of telling a very inspirational story of Walt Disney and the attributes that made him so successful. I highly recommend his book to help motivate you to a future you did not know was possible."

—Don Iwerks
Former Disney Executive, an Oscar Winner and Co-founder of Iwerks Entertainment

"More than 30 years ago, Pat Williams turned a dream into a reality when he guided the efforts to bring the NBA and the Orlando Magic to our city. In *Lead Like Walt*, Pat, a visionary in his own right, gives readers a glimpse into one of the great dreamers of all time, Walt Disney, and the principles and tactics we all can use to make an impact on the lives of others."

—Orlando Mayor Buddy Dyer

"This book is an 'E' ticket if there ever was one. Authors Williams and Denney take you on a real-life Disney adventure through the eyes and experiences of the people who helped the man inside the mouse accomplish a world of wonders.

—Ron Stark
Director of S/R Laboratories® Animation Art Conservation Center
Courvoisier Galleries® of San Francisco

"*Lead Like Walt* is Pat Williams' best thinking on how to be effective in an ever-changing marketplace. It's a page-turner with actionable insights for leaders in any size organization. In fact, I am buying copies for my leaders and friends right away. This is a must-read. Thank you, Pat, for always expanding our minds and engaging our hearts to lead differently."

—Simon T. Bailey
Author of *Be the Spark: Five Platinum Service Principles to Keep Customers for Life*

"Great leaders turn visions into reality by empowering, inspiring, and motivating people. Walt Disney was a great leader. In *Lead Like Walt*, Pat Williams has broken down the essentials of Walt Disney's leadership style, so that all of us can learn from his example. Whether you lead a scout troop, a corporation, or a nation, the insights in this book will make you a more effective leader."

—Senator George J. Mitchell
Former Chairman of The Walt Disney Company

"A delightful book that illuminates the essential leadership qualities of Walt Disney related through the eyes of Pat Williams, an equally imaginative and insightful leader. Chock full of memorable stories, firsthand experiences, and practical advice on being an exemplary leader regardless of where you are on your own leadership journey."

—Barry Posner, Accolti Professor of Leadership at the
Leavey School of Business, Santa Clara University

To Jon Gordon —
My Best Wishes to
A First Class Leader.
Pat William
2019

In memory of
Diane Disney Miller,
and in gratitude to her family for
sharing with me their memories
of Walt Disney

CONTENTS

Foreword

A Magical Tour of Walt's Life

WE WERE BORN IN SOUTHERN CALIFORNIA and spent a lot of time at Disneyland in our early years. Even after we moved to Fresno, four and a half hours from Anaheim, Mom made a point of regularly driving us to Disneyland, our favorite place to go.

During the drive, we'd sit in the backseat and plan our strategy—Indiana Jones Adventure as soon as the gates opened, then circle back to the Jungle Cruise, then dash to Tomorrowland and hit Star Tours and on and on. We'd have it all figured out—though we almost always underestimated the wait times in line.

We never minded the lines. Just being in Disneyland was a magical experience, even if we had to wait forty-five minutes to board the next ride. As much as we loved Space Mountain and the Matterhorn Bobsleds, we didn't just go for the thrill rides. We always made a point of visiting the classic attractions that Walt Disney dreamed up, such as Great Moments with Mr. Lincoln and the Enchanted Tiki Room.

Of course, there was a lot more to our childhoods than trips to Disneyland. Mom is a high school math teacher (now retired) who speaks English, Spanish, and German. She surrounded our lives with good music, great books, plays, and sports. Mom would also take us to our grandparents' home, where my grandmother had literally thousands of books lining her floor-to-ceiling bookshelves, including every Caldecott Award–winning book ever published.

We had well-rounded childhoods, and we learned to love literature, folk tales, and the arts. Mom encouraged our creativity. Brook especially enjoys writing, and Robin likes to draw. There are few things that inspire our creative impulses more than the creations of Walt Disney.

As we grew up, we both became curious about Walt. Who was this man who had a whole company named after him—and, in fact, entire Magic Kingdoms named after him? What kind of childhood did he come from? What were his early influences? What kind of leader was he? What challenges and obstacles did he face? How did Disneyland come to be built?

We started reading about Walt and the history of his company and the history of Disneyland. We read Pat Williams's previous Disney-related book, *How to Be Like Walt*—a treasury of Disney insight if there ever was one. And now we've read *Lead Like Walt*, which is packed with new stories and insights focused on Walt's amazing leadership example.

One fact seems obvious as we look at Walt's life: He would have accomplished great things no matter what field of endeavor he chose. His early life experiences happened to incline him toward animation and movies and theme parks. If he'd had different early influences but the same character and attitude toward leadership, he could have easily been a great NBA coach, military leader, or American president. Walt's traits—vision, communication skills, people skills, character, competence, boldness, and a serving heart—would have equipped him well as a leader in any arena.

As a leader in the entertainment field, he changed the world for the better. In fact, it's hard to imagine a world without Disneyland and Disney movies. There is so much we can learn about leadership from Walt. Pat Williams and Jim Denney have done us all a service by extracting these lessons from his life.

What are your dreams? What are your goals? How do you want to change the world for the better? Take a magical tour of Walt Disney's life. Learn what it means to lead like Walt.

Then do as he did, and make this world a happier and more magical place.

Brook Lopez   **Robin Lopez**
Milwaukee Bucks   *Chicago Bulls*

Mentored by Walt

I NEVER MET WALT DISNEY, yet I feel I've been mentored by him.

In mid-1986, I moved from Philadelphia to Orlando to kick-start a brand-new NBA franchise, the Orlando Magic. Central Florida, the home of the Walt Disney World Resort, is steeped in the lore and legend of Walt Disney, even though he never lived here.

The more stories I heard about Walt Disney's impact on my new hometown, the more I realized that, in building an NBA team from the ground up, I was attempting to do what Walt had already done many times in his life. When he built his animation studio, when he created Mickey Mouse, when he launched the first full-length animated feature, when he built Disneyland and dreamed of a vastly more ambitious project in Florida, Walt always started with a dream and turned it into a reality.

And he did it through leadership.

I define leadership as the ability to direct and motivate a team of people to achieve extraordinary goals. I wasn't sure my leadership skills were up to the challenge of starting a team, getting the community behind it, funding and building an arena, persuading the NBA to award Orlando a franchise, and packing the arena with fans—but I knew Walt could teach me everything I needed to know. He had passed away two decades earlier, but many of the people Walt had mentored were living in Orlando and working at Walt Disney World. I sought them out and asked them for stories and insights about Walt.

Meanwhile, I read every book I could find about Walt. I made an intense study of his life. Along the way, I discovered what I call The Seven Sides of Leadership, seven key leadership traits that all great leaders must have: Vision, Communication Skills, People Skills, Character, Competence, Boldness, and A Serving Heart. I distilled those seven traits into a formula that I speak and write about, based on the leadership model of Walt Disney. I learned those seven leadership traits from Walt because he demonstrated them in abundance.

My friend Swen Nater, who played basketball for (and became a close friend of) legendary UCLA coach John Wooden, penned these lines about the Seven Sides of Leadership:

> Seven things one must do
> To be a leader right and true:
> Have vision that is strong and clear;
> Communicate so they can hear;
> Have people skills based in love;
> And character that's far above;
> The competence to solve and teach;
> And boldness that has fearless reach;
> A serving heart that stands close by
> To help, assist, and edify.

If you possess the Seven Sides of Leadership, you'll be an effective, successful leader in any field of endeavor. These seven traits are learnable skills. As you'll discover as we examine the leadership life of Walt Disney, no goal is too daunting, no dream is out of reach, for a leader who leads like Walt.

In 2004, in partnership with Jim Denney, I wrote *How to Be Like Walt*—a motivational biography of Walt Disney, covering his entire life and legacy. The book remains in print to this day and at last count had more than 200 Amazon reviews averaging 4.7 out of 5 stars. One of the Disney family members I interviewed for that book was Walt's nephew, Roy E. Disney, the son of Roy O. Disney. After I sent Roy a copy of the completed book, he sent me a handwritten note that I have framed on my office wall: "Dear Pat, thanks for including me in your *terrific* book about Walt! It's *wonderful*! —Roy E. Disney."

While writing *How to Be Like Walt*, I also had the joy of getting to know Walt's daughter, Diane Disney Miller. She put me in touch with members of her family, including many of Walt's grandchildren. The Disney family shared with me priceless insights about Walt.

After *How to Be Like Walt* was published, I sent a signed copy to Diane, and she called me and told me she was thrilled with the book—it had captured the spirit of the man she called "Daddy." Five years after the book was released, I received an invitation to the grand opening of the Walt Disney Family Museum. Diane Disney Miller and the Disney family had built a beautiful tribute to Walt in San Francisco. I wanted so badly to be there, but I wondered if I could justify the time and expense of a Florida-to-California flight for a one-night event.

I showed the invitation to my wife Ruth, who said, "Pat, you need to be there. You've become part of the Disney clan ever since *How to Be Like Walt* came out." Ruth was right. I took her advice and booked a flight to San Francisco.

Arriving at the Presidio, where the Disney Family Museum is housed, was a double treat for me. The Presidio is a former US Army fort at the northern tip of the San Francisco Peninsula. The fort was once commanded by another of my leadership heroes, General John J. "Black Jack" Pershing. The setting is breathtaking, with a commanding view of the Golden Gate Bridge.

The moment I stepped into the museum, I was surrounded by the life and accomplishments of Walt Disney. I spent several hours tracing his career through one exhibit after another. The museum encompasses 40,000 square feet, and I could have easily spent days there. It contains galleries of background art and animation drawings, interactive displays, listening stations, a twelve-foot-wide model of Disneyland (as it appeared circa 1959), and more. A display case in the lobby contains many of the awards Walt earned throughout his career, including his many Academy Awards and the Presidential Medal of Freedom. A state-of-the-art theater shows Disney movies throughout the day, and Walt's backyard steam-powered train, the Carolwood Pacific Railroad, is on display.

As I viewed all the artwork, photographs, and film clips from Disney motion pictures, one word echoed in my thoughts: *leadership*. Here was a man who packed many careers into a life that was tragically cut short at age sixty-five. Through the museum displays, I traced his various careers as a cartoon producer, a live-action feature film producer, a documentary filmmaker, a motion-picture technology inventor (who held numerous patents), a beloved TV host, a theme park impresario, and a producer of Olympic Games events and World's Fair exhibits.

It seemed almost impossible that one man could accomplish so much. But those accomplishments prove that Walt was one of the greatest leaders this world has ever seen. He led the Disney company from its founding in 1923 until his death in 1966, a tenure of about forty-three years. The foundation he laid for his company was so strong and durable that the company has lasted for nearly a century. The imprint of his values and his personality were stamped so indelibly on the company that it has continued to thrive and grow for more than five decades following his death.

Today, The Walt Disney Company is a diversified multinational entertainment company and the world's largest media conglomerate (in terms of revenue)—larger than either NBC-Universal or Warner Media. Walt once sent his brother Roy to New York to beg the ABC television network for money to build Disneyland. Today, Disney *owns* ABC. The name Disney has become synonymous with happiness, because happiness was Walt's product. He brought joy and delight to millions of families around the world.

Those were my thoughts as I walked into the dining room at the Walt Disney Family Museum. I looked across the room, spotted a woman, and instantly thought, "That must be Diane Disney Miller." I had never met her before, though we had talked many times on the phone. The Disney family resemblance was unmistakable. I walked up and introduced myself. Her eyes lit up and she said, "Pat! I'm so glad you came!" And we talked as if we had known each other all our lives. She could not have been more gracious.

Finally, she said, "Where are you sitting for dinner?"

"Well, I don't know. I was going to—"

"Pat, you're sitting with us at the Disney family table."

What an honor! There I was with Diane and her husband Ron Miller and the entire Disney family. They all made me feel right at home. It was a wonderful evening in which several hundred people were gathered in one place to celebrate the life and achievements of

Walt Disney—a kind and generous father and grandfather, a man of extraordinary imagination and genius, and one of the most accomplished leaders of all time.

I flew back to Florida the next day with my mind whirling. Most of my thoughts were about Walt himself, the model leader. This was more than a decade ago. In the years since, I have been reading more about Walt. I've interviewed more people who knew Walt or studied his leadership style. I thought we had said all there was to say about him in *How to Be Like Walt*. How wrong I was! Walt still has so much more to teach us about living a life of leadership and achievement.

That's why I have written this new book about Walt Disney, focused exclusively on his leadership example. I finally get to share all the leadership-related stories and insights I've been gathering since the publication of *How to Be Like Walt*. The principles he lived by while building his entertainment empire are the same principles you and I can use in our leadership lives today. These timeless principles are transferable to any leadership arena, any team, any organization. No matter what your age or level of experience, these insights will enable you to become a more effective, influential, and successful leader.

If you've already read *How to Be Like Walt*, you'll be pleased to know that this new book is packed with recently uncovered stories, fresh insights, and powerful leadership principles that have emerged from my recent exploration of Walt's life.

You may not be a "born leader." That's fine. Neither was I, and neither was Walt. There was nothing about Walt's humble beginnings as a Missouri farm boy that suggested the life of bold leadership he would lead. He learned and earned his leadership role the hard way, through trial and error, through on-the-job experience.

In the next chapter, I'll give you an overview of Walt's life and career, paying special attention to those moments in his life when he learned a crucial leadership lesson or displayed a leadership trait. Then in the following chapters, we'll break down his leadership example into the Seven Sides of Leadership. I think you'll be fascinated to discover how these seven leadership principles fueled Walt's success at various stages of his career.

So turn the page with me and let's discover how to lead—and succeed—like Walt.

1

From Humble Origins to Magical Achievements

On Monday, November 28, 1966, newspapers across the country published a story by Associated Press columnist Gene Handsaker that read:

> Walt Disney turns 65 next Monday—deeply involved as usual in projects ever bigger and more diverse.
>
> But only quiet notice is being taken of the occasion. Disney has been taking it easy since he was hospitalized this month for surgery to remove a lesion from his left lung. He's already back in his office and expects to resume a full work schedule in about a month.
>
> The ever-expanding galaxy of Disney enterprises, ranging from a 27,500-acre Florida amusement center to "people mover" cars for

Disneyland, and perhaps for crowded cities, spun along smoothly in the head man's absence. . . .

In an interview, [Walt Disney said], "There's no magic to my formula. Maybe it's because I just make what I like—good human stories." . . .

On a recent rainy day at his sprawling studio, a thirty-year associate was asked to talk of Disney. "Simplest guy in the world," said the aide. "He has no airs or pretense. Drives his own car. Likes lawn bowling and reading and is crazy about his seven grandchildren." . . .

Others have described him as a complicated man who flies from project to project in his company's private jet but takes time to check burned-out light bulbs and dirty washrooms.[1]

Handsaker went on to describe Walt's many current and future projects: *Blackbeard's Ghost* and *The Jungle Book* were in production. Imagineers were busily expanding Tomorrowland in Disneyland while planning a $33 million Disney ski resort at Mineral King (a project that would later be abandoned). The Disney company had acquired 27,500 acres of Florida real estate (twice the area of Manhattan) for the $100 million Disney World project. Walt also planned to soon break ground for the $17 million campus of California Institute of the Arts.

All of these plans and dreams were being led by one amazing man, a leader who had already transformed the motion picture industry, invented a completely new kind of amusement park, and presented the world with such beloved creations as Mickey Mouse, *Snow White and the Seven Dwarfs*, *Fantasia*, and *Mary Poppins*. What Gene Handsaker didn't know when he wrote that column in late November was that Walt Disney would be dead in mid-December—struck down by cancer just as he was achieving his greatest triumphs as a leader.

We'll never know what Walt might have achieved with another

ten or twenty years. But we do know that he packed an incredible list of accomplishments into the years he was given. Such an amazing leader inspires us all the more when we realize that he started life as a Missouri farm boy who never finished high school.

Floyd Norman began his Disney career as an apprentice artist on *Sleeping Beauty* (1959) and worked as a story artist on Walt's last animated film, *The Jungle Book* (1967). Reflecting on Walt in *Fast Company*, he wrote, "Even with his success, Disney regretted not having a college education.... A totally self-taught tycoon, he could easily have taught business-school graduates a thing or two. He knew his audience better than anyone. He never called them customers. They were his guests.... There was nothing cynical about Walt Disney. He truly believed in his special mix of business and magic. Lucky for us, we believed it as well."[2]

What can we learn about leadership from the life of Walt Disney? Prepare to be astonished and inspired. Have I got a story for you.

Happy Years in Marceline

Walter Elias Disney was born in Chicago on December 5, 1901. His father Elias was a Canadian-born building contractor who had earned a dollar a day as a carpenter at the 1893 Chicago World's Fair (the Columbian Exposition). Elias also built the Disney family home at 1249 Tripp Avenue in Chicago, where Walt was born. Walt's mother Flora, a former school teacher, had a lifelong passion for good books. She taught Walt to read before he entered kindergarten.

Elias Disney was known to be a rigid disciplinarian, yet he deeply loved his wife and children. Walt and his three older brothers respected Elias, but also had their struggles with him. In 1906, Elias moved his family from crime-ridden Chicago to a tranquil forty-five-acre farm outside of Marceline, Missouri.

Walt remembered nothing of his early years in Chicago. His first memories were of the bucolic life of a Missouri farm boy. His rural beginnings seem an unlikely starting point for one of the world's great leaders. Yet as Walt's longtime associate, Harrison "Buzz" Price, told me, "Walt was rooted to reality in Marceline. He grew up there around real people. He lived close to the earth, close to nature. He maintained that farm boy quality all his life."

Walt showed an early aptitude for drawing. A retired physician in Marceline, Dr. L. I. Sherwood, once paid Walt twenty-five cents to draw his prize Morgan stallion. In a 1938 letter to the *Marceline News*, Walt recalled, "One of my fondest childhood memories is of Doc Sherwood. He used to encourage me in my drawing and gave me little presents for my efforts. One time I think he must have held a horse of his nearly all day so that I could draw it. Needless to say, the drawing wasn't so hot, but Doc made me think it was tops."[3]

Walt's father discouraged his artistic ambitions and rebuked him for "wasting time" drawing pictures at the expense of his farm chores and school work. "He just scoffed at me," Walt recalled, "and said that if I was foolish enough to want to become an artist, I should learn the violin. Then I could always get a job in a band if I was in need of money."[4]

While in elementary school, Walt was given the assignment, along with the rest of the class, of observing and drawing a bouquet of flowers. Walt did more than observe—he used his imagination. When the teacher examined his drawing, she sharply admonished him: "Walter, flowers do not have faces!"

The boy's reply: "Mine do."[5]

Walt's childhood on the farm outside of Marceline was happy. The farm animals were his friends. He'd greet them by name every morning, invent stories about them, and draw pictures of them. One fat piglet named Skinny followed him around like a puppy.

When illness made it impossible for Walt's father to keep the farm going, he sold the property and livestock at a loss, including Skinny the pig. Walt wept bitterly as his animal friends were auctioned off. Elias moved his family to Kansas City, Missouri, and the happiest years of Walt's life were over.

Diane Disney Miller recalled that her father never spoke of Kansas City, but he often recalled happy times in Marceline. Only when she became an adult did Diane learn that Walt only lived a few short years in Marceline. She was amazed to learn that he spent most of his boyhood in Kansas City. "I really thought he had spent his whole life [in Marceline] before I was born," she said.[6]

Peter Whitehead, creative director of the Walt Disney Hometown Museum in Marceline, observed that Walt gave the town its identity. "The greatest advocate for Marceline," he said, "was Walt Disney himself... [who said] that the greatest place in the whole world was Marceline, Missouri."[7]

Formative Years in Kansas City

From the sale of the farm, Elias purchased a distribution route for the *Kansas City Star*. He hired delivery boys and made Walt and his brother Roy deliver papers without pay. The winters in Kansas City during Walt's boyhood, among the coldest and harshest on record, left an indelible mark on his soul. In late October 1966, shortly before he learned he had terminal cancer, Walt spoke with Charles Champlin of the *Los Angeles Times* and reflected—candidly but without self-pity—on his bleak Kansas City boyhood:

> I had to get up [at] 3:30 every morning. The papers had to be stuck behind
> the storm doors. You couldn't just toss them on the porch. And in the
> winters there'd be as much as three feet of snow. I was a little guy and I'd
> be up to my nose in snow. I still have nightmares about it.
>
> What I really liked on those cold mornings was getting to the apart-
> ment buildings. I'd drop off the papers and then lie down in the warm
> apartment corridor and snooze a little and try to get warm. I still wake
> up with that on my mind.
>
> On nice mornings I used to come to houses with those big old porches
> and the kids would have left some of their toys out. I would find them
> and play with them there on the porch at four in the morning when it
> was just barely getting light. Then I'd have to tear back to the route again.[8]

Through much of his boyhood, Walt delivered papers before school
and held down an after-school job in addition to his schoolwork. No
wonder he grew up with such an intense work ethic. Though Walt
didn't complain, the abrupt transition from his idyllic life in Marceline
to the trauma of a harsh life in Kansas City left him feeling cheated
out of his childhood. Many years later, he observed rather wistfully,
"Marceline was my only childhood."[9]

Walt rarely spoke of his Kansas City years. The only childhood he
ever mentioned or paid homage to in his films and at Disneyland was
his all-too-brief childhood in Marceline.

Though the Kansas City years were hard years, they were formative.
At Benton Grammar School in Kansas City, Walt met a school chum
named Walter Pfeiffer. The two Walts became fast friends, and Pfeiffer
introduced Disney to Kansas City's world of entertainment, especially

the movie houses and vaudeville stages. At school, Walt blossomed as a performer, entertaining friends with his Charlie Chaplin impressions and the funny stories he told while drawing pictures on a chalkboard. At night, he'd sneak out of the house with Walter Pfeiffer to see silent movies and stage plays.

Pfeiffer introduced Walt to a glittering amusement playland in Kansas City called Electric Park, which featured many of the same kinds of attractions that Disneyland is famed for today—thrill rides, a steam train that circled the park, spectacular fireworks displays, and more. That's what Walt remembered when he said that Disneyland "has that thing—the imagination and the feeling of happy excitement —I knew when I was a kid."[10]

In 1916, when Walt was fourteen, he was one of scores of newsboys invited to see a silent movie version of *Snow White and the Seven Dwarfs* at the Kansas City Convention Hall. The film was shown on four giant screens simultaneously, and the sheer grandeur of the presentation made a deep impact on him. In 1938, a year after Walt released his wildly successful animated version of *Snow White and the Seven Dwarfs*, he wrote a column for the Scripps Howard newspaper chain, in which he recalled:

> I was a dyed-in-the-wool movie fan back in the days when you could really call the movies flickers.... I saw Marguerite Clark in *Snow White and the Seven Dwarfs* when I was a newsboy in Kansas City, and it made such an impression that I'm sure it had a bearing on my choosing the Grimm fairy tale for my first full-length production.[11]

When Walt was fifteen, his father sold the newspaper route. Elias had invested in a jelly-canning firm, the O'Zell Company of Chicago, and he and Flora moved to Chicago, along with Walt's younger sister

Ruth. Walt stayed in Kansas City with his brothers Herbert and Roy. He took a summer job as a "news butcher," selling newspapers, candy, and tobacco to passengers on the train. Walt tipped the railroad men with tobacco products he paid for out of his own pocket, and they let him ride in the cab and blow the steam whistle.

At summer's end, Walt moved in with his parents and sister in Chicago, where he enrolled at the Chicago Academy of Fine Arts. There he studied for a career as a newspaper cartoonist. He also attended McKinley High School (though he didn't graduate), and he worked part-time at the O'Zell Company.

Walt applied for a post office job in the summer of 1918 but was rejected because he was only sixteen. He returned later the same day wearing one of his father's suits. The same postmaster who had rejected his application that morning promptly hired him. This incident tells us a lot about Walt's imaginative approach to solving problems—and his skill as a performer.

On September 4, 1918, Walt was working as a mail carrier at Chicago's Federal Building when he narrowly escaped being killed in a terrorist attack. He was walking through the Adams Street lobby of the Federal Building when a powerful bomb exploded at the Adams Street entrance. Walt witnessed the billowing dust and deafening noise of the blast but was unhurt. The explosion killed four people and injured seventy-five others. One of the dead was Walt's co-worker, William Wheeler. The bombing was blamed on the Industrial Workers of the World (also known as "the Wobblies"), a radical international trade union consisting primarily of Marxist, socialist, and anarchist members.

The bomb exploded near the entrance Walt always used to enter and exit the Federal Building. Had his timing been slightly different that day, the world might never have heard of Walt Disney.[12]

The Laugh-O-gram Disaster

In the closing months of World War I, Walt was turned down by both Army and Navy recruiters because of his age. Determined to serve his country one way or another, he used his artistic skills to alter the birthdate on his passport application and was accepted by the Red Cross ambulance corps. Walt's training with the Red Cross was interrupted by the influenza epidemic of 1918. By the time he recovered from the flu and shipped out for France on November 18, the war had been over for a week. He arrived in Le Havre aboard a converted cattle ship on December 4, the day before his seventeenth birthday.

Walt spent nine months chauffeuring military personnel and trucking relief supplies to towns and villages ravaged by war. He spent his idle time drawing in his sketch book or painting cartoons on his vehicles. He also made pocket change painting fake medals on khaki uniforms so that soldiers could impress the mademoiselles. "That was great fun," he recalled. "About a block away, it looked as though the town was full of Croix de Guerres! But it didn't take the little Maries much time to find out that they were only painted on."[13]

Walt lived frugally in France and sent money home to his mother via American Express. At his request, Flora used some of Walt's money to buy a watch for his sister Ruth.

When Walt returned to the States in 1919, he went to Kansas City, where his brother Roy had arranged a job interview with an advertising agency. Walt had filled his sketchbook with drawings while overseas. That impressive portfolio persuaded the Pesmen-Rubin Commercial Art Studio to hire him as an apprentice advertising artist, creating illustrations for theaters and catalogs. There Walt met fellow artist Ub Iwerks. Ub would not only become Walt's friend and collaborator but also the first artist to draw Mickey Mouse. In 1920, Walt and Ub moved to the Kansas City Film Ad Company, where they first experimented with hand-drawn animation.

As an animator, Walt was self-taught. He learned the basics of animation by reading two books he checked out from the Kansas City Public Library—Eadweard Muybridge's *The Human Figure in Motion* (1901) and *Animated Cartoons: How They Are Made, Their Origins and Development* by Carl Lutz (1920). He used the photographic equipment at the Film Ad Company to make photostatic copies of the books.

In May 1922, Walt founded his own animation studio, Laugh-O-gram Films, Inc. He sold $15,000 of stock to local investors— equivalent to $190,000 today. For a twenty-year-old entrepreneur, Walt was a persuasive salesman. He set up shop in a five-room suite in the McConahay Building on East 31st Street and Forest Avenue. In spite of the sale of stock, Walt was undercapitalized and unduly optimistic. He overspent on office space, camera equipment, and staff salaries. He had a lot to learn about leadership, and he would learn it the hard way.

Laugh-O-gram's cartoons put an updated twist on classic fairy tales—*Little Red Riding Hood, Jack and the Beanstalk, Goldilocks and the Three Bears,* and more. Walt's cartoon series was popular with moviegoers, but when his distributor went bankrupt, Walt was forced to lay off employees and cut the pay of his artists. He gave up his apartment, slept on a couch at the office, and took his baths at the Union Station. His meals consisted of cold beans eaten straight from the can.

In 1923, Walt threw in the towel. Laugh-O-gram Films, Inc., filed for bankruptcy. Walt had failed in his first business venture.

A Fresh Start in Hollywood

Walt decided to move to Hollywood, the hub of the motion picture industry, and start over. The bankruptcy court allowed him to keep his movie camera and an unfinished film—the only print of *Alice's Wonderland*, the first film in a series he called The Alice Comedies. Brimming with optimism, he treated himself to a first-class train ticket and arrived in California with a cardboard suitcase and forty dollars in his wallet. He later reflected:

> I think it's important to have a good hard failure when you're young because it teaches you so much. I learned a lot out of that. Because it makes you kind of aware of what can happen to you. That such a thing can happen to anybody, and once you've lived through the worst, you're never quite as vulnerable afterward.
>
> Because of it, I've never had any fear in my whole life when we've been near collapse and all of that. I've never been afraid. I've never had the feeling I couldn't walk out and get a job doing something.[14]

Walt arrived in Los Angeles in July 1923 and moved into a room he rented for five dollars a week from Robert Disney, his uncle, who lived on Kingswell Avenue in the Los Feliz section of L.A. After settling in, Walt went to visit his brother Roy, who was recovering from tuberculosis at the Veterans Hospital in Sawtelle (West L.A.).

At first, Walt wanted to quit the animation business and become a live-action movie director. He recalled in a 1959 interview, "I thought the cartoon business was established in such a way that there was no chance to break into it. So I tried to get a job in Hollywood, working in the picture business."[15] But after every studio slammed its door in his face, he decided to stick with what he knew best: animated cartoons.

Walt's Uncle Robert let him use the garage next to the house as a studio. Walt set up a second-hand camera on an animation stand he built from scrap lumber and dry-goods boxes. It was a primitive arrangement, but Walt completed *Alice's Wonderland*, performing all the animation and camera chores himself in that tiny twelve-by-eighteen garage. (In 1984, the garage that served as Walt's first California studio was moved to the Stanley Ranch Museum in Garden Grove, not far from Disneyland.)

Walt sent his only copy of *Alice's Wonderland* to Margaret Winkler of M. J. Winkler Productions. His Uncle Robert, meanwhile, urged him to get out of the movie business and find a paying job. But Walt couldn't be dissuaded from his goals. On October 8, 1923, he cleared all his equipment and supplies out of Uncle Robert's garage and moved three blocks down Kingswell Avenue. He set up his new studio in the back of the Holly-Vermont Realty office, which he rented for ten dollars a month.

A few days later, Walt rushed to the Veterans Hospital to see Roy. It was almost midnight when Roy awoke to find Walt standing over him, waving a piece of paper. It was a contract, offering Walt $1,500 each for six cartoons.

"Margaret Winkler wants the Alice Comedies," Walt said. "Can you help me get this thing started?"

Roy questioned Walt. Could he deliver the cartoons on time? Had he figured out his costs and profit margins? Walt said yes—and Roy agreed to give Walt the loan he needed. Roy gave Walt $200 and he persuaded a reluctant Uncle Robert to lend Walt an additional $500.

On October 16, 1923, Walt signed the contract with Winkler. That date is observed as the founding of The Walt Disney Company.

Walt completed two Alice Comedies in the back of the realty office at 4651 Kingswell Avenue. In February 1924, he rented a more spacious storefront next door, at 4649 Kingswell, fired himself as an animator, and began hiring artists to take over the animation chores. In a 1949 interview, he recalled, "I've been an artist for thirty years, but there are guys in the studio who can draw rings around me. I never did anything [as an artist] that really satisfied me.... Long ago I discovered moviemaking is no one-man game."[16]

Early in 1925, Walt placed a classified ad in the *Los Angeles Times*: "HELP WANTED: Young lady for ink tracing work. Must have steady hand. Must live in Hollywood. Apply DISNEY BROS. STUDIO, 4649 Kingswell Ave."[17] One of the applicants for the ink artist position was a young woman who recently arrived from Idaho named Lillian Bounds. She got the job. By July of that year, Walt and Lillian were married.

In January 1926, the Disney brothers moved their growing studio to 2719 Hyperion Avenue in Los Angeles. At Roy's insistence, they renamed the company Walt Disney Studios. Roy felt that Walt, the creative half of the team, should be the face of the company.[18] The world took no notice of that little startup. But today, the company Walt and his brother Roy founded in the rented backroom of a realty office is the largest entertainment conglomerate in the world, with annual revenue approaching $60 billion and assets approaching $100 billion.

By mid-1927, Walt felt the Alice Comedies had run their course. Margaret Winkler had retired from the distribution work, and the company was now run by her husband, Charles B. Mintz. Walt and Ub Iwerks (who had moved to California to join Walt's new venture) created a new character, Oswald the Lucky Rabbit. Walt didn't realize that his contract with Mintz ceded ownership of Oswald to the distributor. In 1928, Mintz took Oswald away from Walt, along with many of Walt's top animators.

Walt needed a new character to replace Oswald. Ub Iwerks' son, Don Iwerks, told me that Walt assigned Ub to create the first drawing of Walt's new character, Mickey Mouse. "My dad drew the early animations," Don said, "and Walt became the voice of Mickey. My dad was occasionally asked if he was upset that Walt always got the credit for Mickey Mouse. He responded, 'Anyone can create something. It's what you do with it that counts. Walt did something with Mickey Mouse that made him world-famous.'"

Starting Over—Again

Walt continued to innovate. Mickey's first release, *Steamboat Willie*, was the first cartoon with music, voices, and sound effects synchronized to the action. *Steamboat Willie* debuted at the Colony Theatre in New York City on November 18, 1928. The Walt Disney Company now celebrates that date as Mickey's official birthday.

Not only were Mickey's screen antics highly profitable for the Disney studio, but Mickey-related merchandise became a major source of revenue, keeping the Disney company profitable during the depths of the Great Depression. In 1932, Walt and Roy hired Herman "Kay" Kamen to establish Disney Enterprises, the studio's licensing division. The result was an array of Mickey Mouse watches, books, writing pads, model train sets, and more. In 1934, one of the worst years of the Great Depression, Disney cartoons earned more than $600,000; Disney merchandise added $300,000 more.

In 1929, Walt introduced a new series called Silly Symphonies, which became a proving ground for technical and artistic innovation. The Silly Symphonies introduced popular new characters, including the Three Little Pigs and Donald Duck. On July 30, 1932, Disney released *Flowers and Trees*, the first animated cartoon in Technicolor. The film won the first Academy Award for Animated Short Subjects.

Roy had initially opposed producing cartoons in Technicolor. Color artwork took more time to produce, and special paints had to be mixed that would not chip off the animation cels. Color film stock was much more expensive than black-and-white. But Walt brilliantly used Roy's opposition to color as leverage to wring an important concession from the executives at Technicolor Corporation. "Roy says color is going to cost us a lot of money that we'll never get back," Walt told them. "So if we take a chance on it, you've got to assure us that every other cartoon producer isn't going to rush into the theaters with Technicolor."[19] The company granted Walt a two-year exclusive right to make animated cartoons with the Technicolor process, giving Walt a huge edge over his monochrome rivals.

Walt was always thinking ahead, anticipating trends, and adjusting his strategy accordingly. By the early 1930s, he realized that the market for animated shorts would eventually disappear. He once told an interviewer that he wanted to make feature-length films not merely for the artistic challenge, but as a matter of survival. "I knew we'd have to get off the tail end of the bill," he said. "You could see that pretty soon there wasn't going to be any tail end, only double bills."[20]

In 1934, Walt put his animators to work on the first full-length animated feature. Walt's brother Roy and wife Lillian begged him to stick to animated shorts. They warned him that his obsession with feature-length motion pictures would bankrupt the studio. But Walt believed that in an ever-changing marketplace there was no safety in the status quo. Yes, innovation is risky, but not as risky as stagnation. So Walt plunged his studio into its most ambitious project yet—*Snow White and the Seven Dwarfs*.

One of the most important innovations to come from *Snow White* was the invention of the multiplane camera, which enabled animation to take place in a three-dimensional environment. Primitive versions of the multiplane camera had been used by other filmmakers. Ub Iwerks, who left the Disney studio in 1930 and returned in 1940, built a limited multiplane camera in 1933 out of parts from an old Chevrolet.

But it was Disney engineer William Garity, working under Walt's direction, who built the sophisticated seven-plane camera system that revolutionized animation. Walt unveiled his new technology with the 1937 release of the Silly Symphonies short *The Old Mill*. He used the new camera technology to great effect in *Snow White* and was awarded patent #2,201,689 for the multiplane camera on May 21, 1940.

Walt bet his entire studio on the success of *Snow White and the Seven Dwarfs*. Entertainment and financial experts, meanwhile, dubbed the project "Disney's Folly." Walt sank everything he had into the project and went neck-deep in debt. If the movie failed, the Disney studio would be ruined. But when *Snow White* debuted on December 21, 1937 at the Carthay Circle Theatre in Los Angeles, Walt's creative vision was vindicated. "Disney's Folly" was a box-office smash, bringing in millions and enabling Walt to open a vast new studio complex in Burbank in 1940.

Walt found success at the same time America was sinking into the morass of the Great Depression. Many who had invested in Wall Street lost everything. But Walt didn't invest in stocks and bonds. He invested in himself, his studio, and his dreams. At the same time Wall Street was tanking and banks were failing left and right, the Disney studio was thriving and growing. But the good times at the Disney studio wouldn't last.

The War Years

With the completion of the new Burbank studio, Disney's staff swelled to more than a thousand artists, writers, musicians, and technicians. His studio rolled out a string of feature-length films. Some were commercial failures at the time, including *Pinocchio*, *Fantasia*, and *Bambi*. Others, like *Dumbo*, were wildly successful. All have become entertainment treasures that have stood the test of time.

With his new Burbank studio, Walt believed he had created a utopian artists' community. Every artist had a desk next to a large window with a northern exposure. The studio also provided a gym, showers, volleyball courts, and a baseball field. Walt even planned to build apartments at the studio grounds—a resident artists' colony.

But the box-office failures of *Pinocchio* and *Fantasia*, combined with the outbreak of World War II in Europe, threw a wrench into Walt's utopian dream. The closing of European markets forced belt-tightening and layoffs at the Disney studio. Many Disney artists chafed under a compensation structure in which master animators made as much as $300 a week while inkers and in-betweeners were paid as little as $12 a week. Walt didn't grasp the growing dissatisfaction in his organization until it erupted in an animators' strike on May 29, 1941. The strike would last five weeks, in the midst of the production of *Dumbo*.

During the strike, Walt, Lillian, and fifteen artists went on a three-week goodwill tour of Latin America. The trip was suggested by Nelson Rockefeller, White House Coordinator for Inter-American Affairs. The Franklin D. Roosevelt administration believed Walt could help counter growing influence by Nazi Germany in Latin America—and Walt saw an opportunity to gather ideas for future films. Before leaving on the tour, Walt explained, "While half of this world is being forced to shout 'Heil Hitler,' our answer is to say, '*Saludos Amigos.*'"[21]

One of the many benefits of the tour was the inspiration for Donald Duck's new costar, a *papagaio* (Brazilian parrot) named José Carioca. At one stop in Belém, Brazil, Walt and his traveling companions (collectively nicknamed "El Grupo") were mobbed by school children. Story artist Bill Cottrell observed, "They might not have known who the president of their own country was, but they all knew Walt Disney."[22] The El Grupo party took a thirty-mile steamer cruise up a river in the Colombian rain forest, which eventually inspired the Disneyland attraction, The Jungle Cruise.

While Walt was away, his brother Roy and legal counsel Gunther Lessing settled the animators' strike. To Walt, the strike was an act of betrayal by ungrateful employees, fomented by Communists. Before the strike, Walt had viewed his community of artists as a family, but the strike changed Walt. He would never again feel as close to his artists as he once had.

The World War II era became an artistic wasteland for Walt. More than a quarter of Walt's employees left the studio to join the armed forces. The Disney studio was designated a strategic defense industry by the government, and more than three-quarters of the studio's production was commissioned by the government for the war effort. Most of the films Disney produced during the war were designed as public morale boosters or as training films for the armed forces. The studio produced more than 400,000 feet of film (a total of about sixty-eight hours) for the war effort.

Disney cartoons such as *The New Spirit* (1942) and *The Spirit of '43* (1943) used Donald Duck to encourage Americans to pay their taxes. *Victory Through Air Power* (1943) educated the American public on the strategic value of air warfare. Cartoon shorts such as *Reason and*

Emotion (1943), *Der Fuehrer's Face* (1942), *Education for Death: The Making of a Nazi* (1943), and *Commando Duck* (1944) denounced the evils of the Nazi menace and encouraged sacrifice and rationing to support the war effort. At Walt's direction, most of these films were made at cost, with no margin of profit. The last thing Walt wanted to be was a war profiteer.

But Walt was deeply frustrated that his feature-length projects had to be put on hold and that his studio was forced to produce quantity at the expense of quality. Animation had to be rushed. Artistic flourishes such as multiplane camera zooms and pans could no longer be used. Walt resented the economizing measures the war effort imposed on his studio, but his brother Roy loved it, telling an interviewer from *Fortune* magazine, "I really believe that Walt is beginning to know what a dollar is."[23]

Disneyland and Beyond

The end of World War II rejuvenated Walt. His studio was no longer just a movie factory for the war effort, and Walt was free to return to his pre-war role. An apt title for Walt's position in the company could have been Chief Visionary and Master Innovator. Walt's forward-thinking ideas had propelled the company's fortunes since the very beginning.

Walt pioneered fully synchronized sound cartoons in 1929, the first full-color animated cartoon in 1932, the merchandising of Mickey Mouse also in 1932, the multiplane camera in 1937, the first full-length animated feature in 1937, and an optical printer in 1945 that could combine live action and animation more seamlessly than ever before (it would be used effectively in such films as *The Three Caballeros* and *Mary Poppins*). But Walt, the master innovator, was just getting started.

With feature film production in full swing, Walt turned his thoughts toward a long-cherished dream—an idea he first called Mickey Mouse Park but would eventually be known as Disneyland. When Disneyland opened in 1955, it was unique in all the world. There had been other amusement parks, of course—but nothing like Disneyland. Though Walt's critics had derided Disneyland as a "kiddie park" out in the middle of the orange groves, Disneyland was no "kiddie park." It was a place where parents and children could share fun, imaginative, and educational experiences together. Everything about Disneyland was an innovation straight from the mind of Walt Disney.

Walt didn't invent the idea of a steam train chugging around the park—that idea was inspired by Electric Park in Kansas City from Walt's boyhood days. But it was Walt's innovative idea to put his railroad atop a raised berm that shut the outside world from view. And it was Walt's innovative idea to build an elaborate train station as part of Main Street USA.

It was Walt's innovative idea to have a single entrance into Disneyland. Amusement park operators told him he needed multiple entrances to move people through the gates efficiently, but Walt wanted to control "the show"—the sights of Main Street, the musical soundtrack, the smells from the popcorn stands and candy shop. He didn't just want to pack the customers in. He wanted to give his guests an emotional experience, a feast for the senses. He even "themed" the trash cans, giving them a bamboo theme in Adventureland, a rustic wooden theme in Frontierland, and so forth, so that they blend in as part of the show.

After the park opened, Walt talked to his guests and observed their behavior. He even allowed his guests to help him design and alter Disneyland in subtle ways—especially the flow of foot traffic through the park. Many of the paved pathways in today's Disneyland were bare dirt during Disneyland's first year of operation. Walt deliberately left much of Disneyland unpaved in those early months and let people make their own paths. He told his staff, "The guests will show us where they want to walk."[24]

It was Walt's innovative idea to transform an amusement park into a magical place that is friendly, clean, safe, and reassuring. Amusement park operators told him he could never make money that way. Walt was determined to prove them wrong—and he did. When *Wired* magazine asked Ray Bradbury to describe what the city of the future should look like, he replied, "Disneyland. They've done everything right: It has hundreds of trees and thousands of flowers they don't need, but which they put in anyway. It has fountains and places to sit. I've visited thirty or forty times over the years, and there's very little I would change."[25]

Yet Walt himself was constantly changing Disneyland. Always improving, always innovating, Walt unveiled new futuristic attractions in 1959—the Disneyland Monorail and the Matterhorn Bobsled, the world's first enclosed steel roller coaster (and a forerunner of Space Mountain and the Big Thunder Mountain Railroad). In 1963, Walt opened the Enchanted Tiki Room at Disneyland and introduced a new technology to the world: Audio-Animatronics. In 1964, he invented "switch-back lines," waiting queues that folded in on themselves, taking up less space than straight lines. He also introduced interactive queues with entertaining sights for guests to enjoy while waiting to enter an attraction.

The last great innovation Walt envisioned was something he called "the city of the future" or the "Experimental Prototype Community of Tomorrow" (EPCOT). Walt envisioned a fully planned community, with a high-density urban center (offices, hotels, shopping centers, entertainment venues) surrounded by concentric rings of neighborhoods and parks, without private cars, but fully served by all-electric PeopleMovers and Monorails. He even envisioned the city as having a transparent dome, so that the environment could be comfort-controlled 365 days a year.

Unfortunately, Walt died before he could set this ambitious project in motion. Without Walt's leadership to drive it, his vision of EPCOT had to be abandoned. Instead of Walt's city of the future, Epcot (no longer an all-caps acronym) became a theme park, Disney's second Florida theme park built after the Magic Kingdom. Epcot is a wonderful theme park, with its trademark geodesic Spaceship Earth, its Future World attractions, and its World Showcase pavilions. But it's only a theme park, not the Community of Tomorrow Walt envisioned.

Someday, the world may catch up to Walt's amazing utopian dreams. He was an extraordinary innovator. He was a visionary with an uncanny ability to peer into the future and see possibilities no one else saw—and a leader who turned those possibilities into realities. Yet at heart Walt was still a farm boy from Marceline, Missouri. From the humblest of origins, Walt appeared on the scene, weaving wonder and achieving magical goals.

In the next seven chapters, we will focus on the seven leadership traits that enabled Walt to astonish the world, again and again. As you discover the secrets of Walt's leadership greatness, I think you'll be inspired as I was. I used these leadership insights to help build an NBA franchise next door to Walt Disney World.

How will *you* use these insights? What is *your* leadership dream? Are you ready to learn Walt's principles of magical leadership?

Are you ready to astonish the world?

2

Walt's Vision

WHATEVER YOU'VE HEARD ABOUT THE ORIGIN OF DISNEYLAND is wrong.

Walt once said, "Disneyland really began when my two daughters were very young. Saturday was always Daddy's Day, and I would take them to the merry-go-round and sit on a bench eating peanuts while they rode. And sitting there, alone, I felt there should be something built, some kind of family park where parents and children could have fun together."[26]

That's the official Disneyland origin story, as Walt himself told it. If you go to the Main Street Opera House in Disneyland, you'll see a green park bench with an inscription that reads: "The actual park bench from the Griffith Park Merry-Go-Round in Los Angeles, where Walt Disney first dreamed of Disneyland."

But while it's true that Walt spent many hours on that Griffith Park bench, planning and dreaming about Disneyland, Walt's Disneyland dreams predate that bench by many years. In fact, Walt was thinking about building his own theme park years before he invented Mickey Mouse. My writing partner, Jim Denney, uncovered the *real* Disneyland origin story and published his findings at the MouseInfo.com website in August 2017.[27]

The key to Walt's Disneyland vision, Jim said, is the fact that Walt had *two* childhoods—a happy childhood on the farm near Marceline, Missouri, and a miserable childhood in Kansas City. Walt's few years on that Missouri farm defined his life. He paid tribute to his Marceline years in films about small-town America (*So Dear to My Heart*, *Pollyanna*, and *Lady and the Tramp*, for example). Walt's happy Marceline years are also enshrined in Disneyland's Main Street USA, which depicts an idealized small American town in 1910, the year Walt's happy Marceline childhood ended.

But Kansas City is where Walt discovered a place called Electric Park. That amusement park was a bright spot in Walt's bleak Kansas City boyhood. Located at 46th Street and the Paseo, Electric Park featured band concerts, a merry-go-round, boat rides, a roller coaster, and other thrill rides. An old-fashioned steam train carried passengers around Electric Park and fireworks lit up the night skies. It's easy to see where Walt's inspiration for Disneyland came from.

But there are big differences between Electric Park and Disneyland. First, there's a difference of scale—Electric Park's fifteen acres versus the 160 total acres of Disneyland. Electric Park in Walt's day occupied about the same space as Adventureland plus New Orleans Square in today's Disneyland. And Walt's vision for Disneyland included themed lands (Adventureland, Frontierland, Fantasyland, Tomorrowland), a towering central castle, and so much more.

Though admission to Electric Park was just ten cents, Walt couldn't afford a ticket. In an interview with Keith Gluck of The Disney Project, Diane Disney Miller said her father's older brother Herbert Disney (or perhaps Herb's girlfriend) showed Walt and his sister Ruth how to sneak into Electric Park. Diane added that her father told Ruth, "I'm going to have one of these [amusement parks] someday, but mine's going to be clean."[28] Walt was fifteen or younger when he confided these plans to Ruth. Walt kept the dream of a clean family amusement park in his heart for four decades.

The Unstoppable Vision

When Walt began serious preparation for Disneyland in the late 1940s and early 1950s, everyone opposed it. His brother and business partner Roy, his wife Lillian, the amusement park operators he consulted, the top network brass at NBC and CBS—all told him that Disneyland was doomed to failure. Entertainment experts dubbed the idea "Disney's Folly" (they had said the same thing about Snow White and the Seven Dwarfs two decades earlier).

Walt's Disneyland vision was deeply personal. Main Street USA recreated Walt's boyhood in Marceline. Fantasyland was based on stories he loved as a boy. Frontierland was rooted in his love of the past. Tomorrowland was built on his fascination with the future. Disneyland is derived from Walt's golden moments in Marceline and his stolen moments at Electric Park.

To Walt, Disneyland wasn't merely a bold commercial venture. It was his boyhood dream and his grown-up obsession. By building Disneyland, Walt kept a promise he had made to himself as a boy. That's why Disneyland was so important to Walt. That's why no one could talk him out of it—not even his brother Roy.

Roy O. Disney had always found ways to finance Walt's dreams. It was Roy who enabled Walt to start over in 1923 after the bankruptcy of Laugh-O-gram in Kansas City. It was Roy who had found the financing to complete *Snow White and the Seven Dwarfs* in 1937. It was Roy who settled the 1941 animators' strike and kept the Disney studio afloat during the lean years of World War II.

But Roy refused to lift a finger for Disneyland. He had three sound business reasons: (1) Walt Disney Productions was a motion picture studio. An amusement park would be a distraction from the company's proven business model. (2) Nobody in the company had ever operated an amusement park before. The company lacked the competency to succeed in such an undertaking. (3) Walt's Disneyland obsession was so expensive it could bankrupt the company.

Walt, however, had sound business reasons on his side as well. He no longer saw Walt Disney Productions as merely a movie studio but as an *entertainment company*. From the beginning, Walt had steadily increased the scope of his vision for the studio. It began as a cartoon factory, then (over Roy's objections) it became an animated feature film studio, then (over Roy's objections) it became a live-action movie studio. To Walt, it was only natural for the company to conquer new worlds of entertainment. The lack of experience in running an amusement park could be overcome by studying other parks and hiring experts and consultants.

But Walt didn't have an answer for Roy's third objection: money.

Walt had always been the creative and visionary half of the Disney brothers' partnership. Roy's job was to fund Walt's visions. But if Roy refused to help fund Disneyland, Walt's dream was dead in the water. The Disney brothers were at an impasse over Disneyland, but Walt refused to surrender his vision. Averaging four or five hours of sleep per night, he spent his waking hours planning the park and thinking up schemes to finance it.

One of Walt's least likely ideas proved to be the key to Roy's heart. Former Disney president Card Walker got the story straight from Walt. Walker said that Walt "did a lot of funny things to needle Roy, to make sure that Roy understood how serious he was about going forward with [Disneyland]. Like one time when he told Hazel George, our nurse, 'I'm not getting anyplace with the financial people. . . . Now, you go around and get the different people at the Studio to make commitments. Like, "I'll commit $10 or $100," something that ridiculous, Walt was smart enough to know that wasn't the answer [to financing the park]. . . . But it was the needle."[29]

And Roy felt the needle. Hazel assembled an informal group of investors called the Disneyland Backers and Boosters. The money they raised was a pittance compared to the need. But when Roy saw that Walt's employees believed in his vision, his own opposition softened—exactly as Walt had planned.

In March 1952 (apparently after Hazel George formed the Disneyland Backers and Boosters), Roy wrote a memo to Walt which read, in part, "I don't see it clearly yet, but I do think the idea [of an amusement park] should be considered and studied on its merits."[30] That year, Roy allocated $10,000 to develop plans for Disneyland. It was a baby step, but Walt was cheered that Roy was taking *any* steps at all.

Designing and Refining the Vision

On December 16, 1952, Walt founded Walt Disney, Inc. (It was later renamed WED Enterprises after the initials for Walter Elias Disney; WED was later renamed Walt Disney Imagineering, Inc.). WED was an engineering company with one purpose: to design and build Disneyland. Walt coined a new job title for his WED engineers: "Imagineers" (a portmanteau of "imagination" and "engineers").

WED Enterprises was Walt's company—he owned it and called all the shots. WED rented space at Disney's Burbank studio, and Walt recruited talent both within and outside of his studio. Since many Imagineers were longtime Disney artists, none of whom had ever designed an amusement park before, they planned Disneyland the same way they had planned animated cartoons—with "storyboards," corkboards with drawings pinned on them to illustrate a sequence of visual elements. The drawings could be repositioned to test different ideas.

Walt shared the broad vision of Disneyland with his Imagineers, then turned them loose to imagine the possibilities. "The dream is wide open!" he told them.[31] Imagineer Harriet Burns recalled, "I worked in the art department at WED. Walt would come down to work with us. He'd sit on a stool and relax with us because we were so informal. He was always up, always positive. How many CEOs would come down to work with his employees like that?"[32]

Walt was hammering out his boyhood dreams, turning his decades-long vision into reality. He spent long days at WED, suggesting improvements to drawings and three-dimensional models, brainstorming ideas, and inspiring his Imagineers with his vision. After an exhausting day at WED, he'd return to his Carolwood Drive home for dinner. After dinner, he'd retire to the barn behind his home where he'd work on plans long into the night. Disneyland was Walt's day job, his hobby, and his obsession.

He wasn't content to build a conventional Coney Island–style amusement park and decorate it with Disney characters, as the experts advised. He was creating something that had never existed before. He saw Disneyland as a completely immersive experience, a time machine that would transport people to the past, future, or realms of pure imagination. That's why, as you enter Disneyland, you pass under a plaque reading, HERE YOU LEAVE TODAY AND ENTER THE WORLD OF YESTERDAY, TOMORROW, AND FANTASY.

Walt wanted his guests to feel at home in Disneyland, so he laid out the park like a wheel with a hub and spokes. All you had to do was walk up Main Street toward Sleeping Beauty Castle, and you'd find yourself at Central Plaza, the hub. From there, you could take the "spokes" to Adventureland, Frontierland, Fantasyland, or Tomorrowland. The "hub-and-spokes" layout of Disneyland was Walt's innovative idea.

Another of Walt's visionary innovations was the use of forced perspective in constructing Disneyland. As a moviemaker, Walt knew how to create the illusion of height. The buildings of Main Street USA use forced perspective to make them seem taller than they are. The ground floor is seven-eighths scale, the second story is five-eighths scale, and the third story is one-half scale—and the doors, windows, and bricks are scaled accordingly. This same principle is used to psychologically "heighten" Sleeping Beauty Castle and the Matterhorn.

Walt wanted Disneyland to be more than an amusement park. It should be a *show*. The park is divided into two areas, "onstage" (the public area) and "backstage" (the part the public never sees). Disneyland does not have employees—it has "cast members." Everyone the public meets, from the food service worker to the costumed character, is part of the show. Every cast member stays "in character" when talking to guests.

One reason Disneyland seems so perfect in every detail is because Walt had many years to plan it. Though it only took him a year and a day to build Disneyland, he spent the better part of forty years refining his vision.

The Invention of Synergy

In July 1953, Walt commissioned the Stanford Research Institute (SRI) to identify prospective sites for Disneyland. At the top of the list was a sleepy little farm town called Anaheim in Orange County, thirty-five miles south of Los Angeles. The Santa Ana Freeway was under construction, offering ready access to Harbor Boulevard.

That fall, Walt decided to approach the TV industry for funding. Bob Thomas wrote in *Building a Company:*

> The Disneys had considered television as a medium for their pictures ever since the mid-thirties, when they ended their relationship with United Artists because the distributor insisted on retaining the television rights. In 1950 and 1951, Walt had produced special programs for NBC [and CBS], and he was impressed by the huge audiences they drew. All three networks had urged him to produce a weekly series, but he had declined. Disneyland provided the impetus. He figured a network could help him finance the park. And the series would publicize both Disneyland and the theatrical product.[33]

At that time, all other Hollywood filmmakers despised that glowing box in everybody's living room, fearing it would put them out of business. Walt was the only movie mogul who embraced TV. His early adoption of the new medium is evidence of his far-seeing vision.

In fall 1953, Walt and Roy went before the board of directors of Walt Disney Productions and explained Walt's plan for using television to fund and publicize Disneyland. By this time, Walt's enthusiasm for Disneyland had finally infected Roy. The board appointed Roy—once Disneyland's staunchest foe—as salesman for the project.

Roy called NBC to set up a meeting, expecting to have weeks to prepare. But the NBC execs were eager to meet with Roy the very next week. Roy agreed—then realized he had no drawing of Disneyland to show them. The network brass would never grasp Walt's vision unless they could see it. Roy told Walt he needed a detailed rendering of Disneyland—and he needed it Monday.

Walt knew only one artist who could produce an eye-popping rendering on such short notice. Herb Ryman was a longtime artist for MGM (he designed all the architecture and sets for the Emerald City in *The Wizard of Oz*). His Disney career began with such films as *Fantasia* and *Dumbo*. He left the Disney studio in 1944 to work at 20th Century Fox, but he and Walt had remained good friends.

On Saturday morning, September 26, 1953, Walt called Ryman and asked him to come down to the studio.[34] Twenty minutes later, Ryman pulled up at the Buena Vista entrance, where Walt was standing at the gate to meet him. As Walt ushered him into the building, he said, "Herbie, I want to talk to you about an amusement park."

"You mean you're going ahead with this idea of an amusement park across the street?" Ryman knew that Walt had wanted to build Mickey Mouse Park (as the theme park project was then known) on an eight-acre lot adjacent to the Burbank studio, across Riverside Drive.

"No," Walt said, "it's bigger than that." Walt added that he hadn't acquired the land yet but was researching potential sites. "Herbie, my brother Roy has got to go to New York on Monday morning. He's got to talk to the bankers....If we don't have the money, we can't do anything."

When Walt asked Ryman to produce a completed rendering in just two days, Ryman refused. Walt was asking the impossible.

But when Walt promised to stay with Ryman day and night until the drawing was complete, Ryman couldn't say no. They worked together all of Saturday and into Sunday. Walt described his vision in words and showed him the sketches that his WED Imagineers had produced of different parts of the park. Walt communicated his vision with such passion and clarity that Ryman could see it clearly in his own imagination.

In two days, working around the clock, Ryman created a beautiful rendering of Disneyland. It was all there, exactly as Walt had envisioned: the Train Station and Disneyland Railroad, Main Street USA, the Central Plaza, Frontierland (with the *Mark Twain* paddle wheeler), Fantasyland (including the Castle, the Carrousel, and the Pirate Ship), Tomorrowland (with the Moonliner towering over it), and Adventureland (though Ryman had placed the Jungle Cruise in the southeast corner of the park instead of the southwest where it is today).[35] Ryman mounted the three-foot by five-foot artwork on a three-panel presentation board.

On Monday, September 26, Roy took the Disneyland rendering in a carrying case on his flight to New York. There he met with executives of CBS and NBC, showing them Ryman's artwork and passing out a six-page prospectus on the Disneyland TV show and theme park. CBS flatly said no. David Sarnoff, the founder of RCA (parent company of NBC at the time) was interested but passed the negotiation to RCA president Joseph McConnell. Roy found McConnell frustrating to deal with. NBC wanted a Disney TV show—but without the park.

Roy returned to his Waldorf Astoria suite to consider his options. He'd been so sure that either NBC or CBS would agree that he hadn't contacted third-place ABC. Now ABC was his only hope. He called network chief Leonard Goldenson, who had led the restructuring of ABC after its merger with United Paramount Theaters. Goldenson came to Roy's suite and studied the rendering, then read the prospectus. Goldenson agreed on the spot. He later said of Roy, "He was a very good businessman, and not easy to get along with. He bargained for the last cent."[36]

ABC put up $500,000 in cash and cosigned $4.5 million in loans. The network received 34.5 percent ownership of Disneyland, plus the weekly hour-long TV show. The rest of the ownership group would include Walt Disney Productions, Western Printing and Lithographing Company (publishers of Little Golden Books), and Walt himself (a 17.2 percent share). The ownership group assembled $6 million in capital and loan guarantees—far less than the eventual $17 million price tag.

But when the *Disneyland* TV show premiered on Wednesday, October 27, 1954, almost nine months before opening day, the park looked like it was already a roaring success. Corporate sponsors lined up to invest, drawn by Walt's vision. Herb Ryman's ink-and-water color rendering of Walt's vision was the key to everything that followed.

The Ryman map later disappeared and was thought lost, though a redrawn version of the original map has appeared in books on Disneyland over the years. It turns out that Walt gave the original map to a friend, Grenade Curran. A jack of all movie trades, Grenade had worked as a safety diver and stuntman in *20,000 Leagues Under the Sea*, an actor in the *Disneyland* "Davy Crockett" series, a voice actor in *Lady and the Tramp*, and more. Walt, who nicknamed Grenade "Shrapnel," gave him the Ryman map as a gift in late 1955. The map surfaced in 2017 in an auction held by Van Eaton Galleries in Sherman Oaks, selling to an undisclosed bidder for $708,000.

Bruce DuMont, founder of Chicago's Museum of Broadcast Communications, offered this perspective on Walt as a television pioneer:

> Walt realized he had a brand name at the motion-picture box office which was indelibly etched in the culture. Then, along came this new thing called television, and he realized that it would be a phenomenal delivery system for his motion picture business. He also realized that the brand name could be expanded into theme parks. With the television broadcast going into millions of homes, it solidified the association with family entertainment and became the vehicle to promote the theme parks, too. I think that may make him the father of commercial synergy.[37]

I agree. Walt invented synergy when he devised his innovative strategy for funding and popularizing his fantasy playland. I define *synergy* as a system whose parts function together so that the whole is greater than the sum of the parts. Synergy is a way to get more energy out of a system than you put into it.

The system Walt designed consisted of three parts: television (the *Disneyland* TV show), motion pictures (Disney's library of cartoons, documentaries, and feature films), and the theme park (Disneyland). Television advertised Disneyland and Disney movies. The Disney library of motion pictures provided content for television and themes to enhance Disneyland. And Disneyland, in turn, generated awareness of and excitement for Disney movies and the *Disneyland* TV show.

The result was that the whole Disney entertainment universe exceeded the sum of its parts. It was conceived entirely in the visionary mind of Walt Disney. Television tilted the financial playing field in Walt's favor, providing the funding and momentum he needed to build his Magic Kingdom in a year and a day.

The *Disneyland* TV series premiered on ABC on Wednesday, October 27, 1954. In addition to building excitement and expectation for Disneyland, the show also ensured the success of three theatrical films released before Disneyland opened: *20,000 Leagues Under the Sea* (released December 23, 1954), *Davy Crockett, King of the Wild Frontier* (compiled from episodes of the *Disneyland* show and theatrically released May 25, 1955), and *Lady and the Tramp* (released June 22, 1955).

The magic that built Disneyland was not pixie dust or wishing on a star. It was synergy.

A Detailed Vision

In a May 1954 column about Disneyland, journalist Aline Mosby revealed how detailed Walt's vision of his park truly was:

Nearly 500 workers at the Disney studio in Burbank are working on the Disneyland project. In a town where gossip is a chief occupation, it is amazing the intricate project was kept quiet. In three rooms draftsmen bend over their boards, drawing detailed plans for the buildings. Nearly everything at the huge park, including a huge paddleboard river boat that will run on a little lake, will be built at the studio.

She went on to describe Walt's "elevated railway" (the Disneyland Railroad), "a replica of a 1910 town, complete with pony-drawn carriages, restaurants, and shops" (Main Street USA), a river with "alligators and head-hunters" (the Jungle Cruise), the "World of Tomorrow" with a "rocket ship for a 'trip to the moon,'" and "a flight in a sailing ship over a miniature set of the city of London" (Peter Pan's Flight).

One of the most revealing details in Mosby's report was this note: "An overhanging monorail car can whiz visitors over the project." Though the Disneyland Monorail wasn't built until 1959, Walt envisioned it *at least* as early as 1954.[38]

Every detail of Walt's park was important to him. Longtime Disney scriptwriter and Imagineer Marty Sklar recalled the first time he met Walt. "It was two weeks before Disneyland opened, July 1955," he said. "I had been hired to create a newspaper that would be sold on Main Street for ten cents." Sklar was twenty-one, still attending college—and he had to present his concept to Walt himself. Sklar said, "I kept thinking, 'Why does he have time for this little thing I'm doing in the middle of the chaos of finishing his park?' It took me a long time to figure it out, but to Walt, Main Street was a real place, so it needed a real newspaper."[39]

Walt had every detail of his park thought out long before Herb Ryman created the first Disneyland rendering. One detail was Disneyland's shopping district, Main Street USA. Outwardly, Main Street looks like two rows of stores circa 1910—one row on the west side of the street and one on the east. But look closer and you'll discover another Disney innovation. When Disneyland opened, you could step into the Emporium on the west side of the street, then wander into the Glassblower Shop, then stroll into the Upjohn Pharmacy—without ever stepping outside. Walt's Main Street USA was the first indoor shopping mall in the world.

Walt was also a technological visionary. It was his idea to surround an audience with a motion picture. That's the concept behind Circle-Vision 360°, the first fully immersive movie experience in the world. A nine-camera array was mounted atop a car that traveled around America, capturing scenic views in a full 360-degree radius.

The synchronized images were then projected on nine screens surrounding the audience. Audience members could turn and view the film in any direction. The first Circle-Vision 360° film shown at Disneyland in 1955 was *America the Beautiful.*

Walt's vehicle designer Bob Gurr was impressed with Walt's mastery of the details of all of his projects. Gurr flew with Walt to Florida for an aerial view of the Walt Disney World site. "I vividly remember sitting next to Walt on a plane," Gurr said, "when he pointed to the center of EPCOT, an oval-shaped area. He said, 'When EPCOT gets up and running, there's going to be this spot with a little bench. That's where Lilly and I are going to sit and watch.' I thought this was pretty interesting. Walt could see the big picture, but he could also have in mind this little detail. And he knew where his part was going to be within that little detail."[40]

Whenever Walt envisioned a project, he envisioned it in exacting detail.

A Futuristic Vision

If Walt Disney had never been born, Neil Armstrong and Buzz Aldrin might never have landed on the moon. A visionary leader doesn't merely *imagine* the future or *predict* the future. A visionary leader *makes the future happen*—and Walt helped make the Apollo 11 mission to the moon happen.

Walt was a visionary futurist. Walt's friend Ray Bradbury told me about the first time he met Walt Disney. They met in a department store at Christmastime. When Ray introduced himself, Walt said, "Ray Bradbury! I know your books!" Why did Walt know Ray's books, such as *The Martian Chronicles* and *Fahrenheit 451*? Walt knew them because he was a science fiction fan. That's why Walt produced *20,000 Leagues Under the Sea*, and that's why there's a Tomorrowland in Disneyland.

In the early 1950s, while Walt was preparing to build Disneyland, *Collier's* magazine published a series of articles on space travel. Contributors included space scientists Wernher von Braun and Willy Ley. Walt hired von Braun and Ley as consultants for the first Tomorrowland episode of his *Disneyland* series, "Man in Space." The show aired March 9, 1955, and was seen by more than 40 million TV viewers. Suddenly, millions of Americans became excited about humanity's future in space.

A sequel, "Man and the Moon," aired December 28, 1955. Another sequel, "Mars and Beyond," aired December 4, 1957. According to Disney animator Ward Kimball, who directed all three space episodes, President Dwight Eisenhower called Walt the day after "Man in Space" aired, requesting a copy to show senior Pentagon officials.

Eisenhower was enthusiastic about the peaceful exploration of space. He wanted his generals to see rockets as human transportation systems, not merely as delivery systems for nuclear weapons. On July 29, 1958, three years after "Man in Space" debuted, Eisenhower established the National Aeronautics and Space Administration (NASA) as the civilian space agency of the United States. He appointed Wernher von Braun head of NASA's Marshall Space Flight Center in Alabama.

In 1965, von Braun took Walt on a tour of the Marshall Center. Walt promised to use his TV show to "wake people up to the fact that we've got to keep exploring." In *Marketing the Moon*, authors David Meerman Scott and Richard Jurek observe that it was the visionary partnership between Walt Disney and Wernher von Braun that helped launch the human race to the Moon:

Psychologically, Disney and von Braun shared a number of distinct personality traits, the foremost being an unwavering dedication to seeing their personal visions made concrete....

Walt Disney, *Collier's*, and Wernher von Braun played pivotal roles in the preparation [of America for the space age] by envisioning an optimistic future.... In less than a decade, space travel had emerged from the realm of children's adventure stories and the domain of rocketry and science fiction hobbyists to the world of front-page headlines.[41]

Though Walt didn't live to see the July 1969 moon landing, he may have helped save the Apollo 11 mission from failure. Steve Bales, a thirteen-year-old boy living in an Iowa farm town, was watching *Disneyland* on TV shortly after Christmas 1955—the episode titled "Man and the Moon." Bales later said, "This show, probably more than anything else, influenced me to study aerospace engineering."[42]

Bales accepted a summer internship at NASA in 1964. Three months later, NASA hired him as a flight controller, and he served as backup controller for Gemini 3 and 4. Less than two years after being hired, he was the lead guidance officer for Gemini 11 and 12, before moving on to the Apollo program.

At age twenty-seven, Bales was assigned to the most important mission of his career: lead guidance officer for Apollo 11. He was in Houston's Mission Control as astronauts Neil Armstrong and Buzz Aldrin descended toward the moon. When the *Eagle* lander was 33,000 feet above the moon, Armstrong radioed, "Program alarm." This meant the computer was having to perform too many tasks and couldn't keep up—a critical safety issue.

A NASA guidance specialist asked Bales if the landing should proceed or abort. Bales had to make an immediate decision. If he didn't say "go" in less than six seconds, the landing would be aborted. Armstrong and Aldrin would have to turn their backs on the moon and head for home.

Bales radioed CAPCOM (capsule communicator) Charles Duke, saying, "We're *go* on that alarm." Duke relayed the word to Armstrong and Aldrin: "We're *go!*"

Three and a half minutes later, Bales and the rest of the Mission Control team in Houston heard those historic words: "Houston, Tranquility Base here. The *Eagle* has landed."[43]

Consider this: If Walt Disney had not aired "Man and the Moon" on December 28, 1955, it's unlikely that Steve Bales would have been in that critical position, making the critical "go" decision, on July 20, 1969. So Walt deserves at least a footnote in the history books for those boot prints on the moon.

How to Be a Visionary Leader

Walt reportedly explained his visionary leadership this way: "I dream. I test my dreams against my beliefs. I dare to take risks. And I execute my vision to make those dreams come true."[44]

Disneyland vehicle designer Bob Gurr said, "When the Imagineers were locked into a major project, we were each immersed in our own private world. All we could see was the Autopia or the Monorail—whatever project we were working on. After completion, we'd compare notes with each other, and we discovered that Walt had seen the entire picture the whole time. He was the Grand Master of the Vision."[45]

Today it's hard to imagine a world without Disney theme parks. But when Walt was planning Disneyland, he couldn't get the bankers to see the vision he saw. "I could never convince the financiers that

Disneyland was feasible," he said, "because dreams offer too little collateral."[46] What can we learn about visionary leadership from Walt's example? Here are the lessons I've discovered:

1. **Find your obsession.** The dream of a clean, family-friendly magical kingdom seized Walt's imagination when he was a boy. That boyhood vision became his grown-up obsession. Ward Kimball said, "Once he got this bug about the park, it was an obsession. That's all he thought about."[47]

   Walt's obsession cost him many sleepless nights—but he always put his insomnia to good use. When he couldn't sleep, he'd analyze his problems and dream up creative solutions. One sleepless night in early 1953, an idea came to him: *television.* The TV networks had the money Walt needed, and he had the film library the networks wanted. The *Disneyland* TV series was born out of Walt's restless obsession with building his Park.

2. **Listen to sound advice but ignore the naysayers.** In July 1953, Walt commissioned the Stanford Research Institute (SRI) to advise him on the best sites for Disneyland. SRI's Buzz Price studied population trends, infrastructure and transportation trends, climate and weather, and other factors, then advised Walt to build his park in Anaheim. Buzz Price was one of the few people who shared Walt's vision and believed in it.

   In November 1953, Price joined Disney execs Dick Irvine and Nat Weinkoff at an amusement park convention in Chicago. The three Disney representatives met privately with four amusement park operators at the Drake Hotel: William Schmitt (Riverview Park, Chicago), Harry Batt (Pontchartrain Beach Park, New Orleans), Ed Schott (Coney Island, Cincinnati), and

George Whitney (Playland at the Beach, San Francisco). Walt's representatives unrolled a photostatic copy of Herb Ryman's Disneyland map and taped it to the wall. Walt wanted to know what industry experts thought of his plan.

The experts declared that Walt was doing everything wrong. There were no roller coasters or Ferris wheels, no carnival midway games, and no beer sales. Building custom-themed rides would cost a fortune versus the mass-produced rides found in every other amusement park. Walt's Park contained many features (like the Castle and the Town Square) that would produce no revenue. And forget about keeping the park clean! Walt's Park, the experts said, was a bankruptcy waiting to happen.

Walt considered the views of the experts, weighing them against his own instincts and SRI's research. Then he proceeded to build Disneyland and prove the experts wrong. By 1957, after two-and-a-half years of operation, the park had welcomed more than 10 million visitors. The experts had also mistakenly thought that Walt was building a "kiddies playland" in Anaheim, but of those 10 million visitors, adults outnumbered children by more than three to one.[48]

The experts were completely wrong about Disneyland because they didn't understand that Walt was completely reinventing the amusement park. The average stay time in an ordinary amusement park was two hours or less. People would tire of the noise and dirtiness, and they'd leave. Historian Greg Van Gompel observed that Walt "created an environment with an ambiance that was so refreshing and pleasant" that people would stay all day. Longer stays meant more money spent on attractions, food, and souvenirs.[49]

Ray Bradbury told me, "Everything Walt achieved in his life was something he was told he couldn't do. His father told him he could never make a living by drawing cartoons. He spent his entire career proving the doubters wrong. And he had a wonderful time doing it." Listen to the experts—but when you're convinced your vision is right and the experts are wrong, trust your vision.

3. **Delegate, but don't abdicate.** Delegating means assigning tasks and responsibilities to other people and holding them accountable for the results. Walt was a master delegator. He delegated chores, but he didn't abdicate his responsibility for the final result. He oversaw every detail of every cartoon and feature film—and he knew the Disneyland blueprints by heart.

Ward Kimball recalled that Walt "walked over every inch of Disneyland, telling them to move a fence a little more to the left because you couldn't see the boat as it came 'round the corner. I'd be with him out there, and he'd say, 'The lake is too small. Maybe we should make it larger. Let's find out if we can move the train wreck over another fifty feet.'"[50] Walt once told Kimball, "My fun is working on a project and solving the problems. If I just sit in the office and okay drawings...what fun is that?"[51]

Walt had an army of people designing and building Disneyland. He didn't have to be on-site day after day. But he wanted to be there, inspiring his people, inspecting their work, and watching his dream take shape. Being personally involved in every detail of Disneyland brought joy to Walt's soul. At the WED Enterprises shop, where his Imagineers were building attractions for Disneyland, he told Imagineer Marc Davis, "I love it here. WED is just like the Hyperion studio used to be in the days when we were always working on something new."[52]

4. **Be 100 percent committed to your vision.** Walt wouldn't let anyone stand in his way, not even his brother Roy. When Roy refused to allocate funds for Disneyland, Walt emptied his savings account, borrowed $100,000 against his life insurance, sold his Smoke Tree Ranch vacation home, and hocked every scrap of collateral he owned. That's 100 percent commitment.

The night before Disneyland opened, what was Walt doing? He was working alongside Imagineer Ken Anderson in the *20,000 Leagues Under the Sea* walk-through exhibit, spray-painting the backdrop behind the giant squid. Walt did not lead from an ivory tower. He was a visionary who got in the trenches with his troops. Walt was all-in.

5. **Find your "dreaming tree."** When Walt was five, his mother held him back from school and taught him to read. She wanted Walt and his little sister Ruth to start school at the same time so he could look after her. As a result, Walt and Ruth spent many carefree days tramping the hills or lying in the shade of a giant cottonwood tree.

Under that ancient tree, Walt practiced what he called "belly botany,"[53] lying very still on his stomach and observing the insects, birds, lizards, squirrels, and other animals that crawled or skittered around him. He once said, "I drew whatever we saw. I could always count on rabbits and squirrels and field mice. And on a good day, sometimes Bambi came by."[54] He also daydreamed under that tree, imagining stories about the animals he saw, picturing them dressed up in clothes, talking and having adventures.

Walt called that cottonwood tree his "Dreaming Tree." It's the place where he absorbed inspiration from nature and daydreamed about the future. As an adult, he returned several times to Marceline, and he'd always spend time under the Dreaming Tree, remembering the happiest days of his life. He'd come away inspired with new ideas and visions.

Walt's original Dreaming Tree suffered from disease and lightning strikes, and finally toppled during a wind storm in 2015. However, a sapling from the Dreaming Tree was planted on the farm in September 2004, so the Dreaming Tree lives on.

What is your Dreaming Tree? Where do you absorb inspiration and see visions of the future? Every leader should have a favorite park bench, a favorite seat in the chapel, or a patch of grass in the backyard—a place you call your Dreaming Tree.

Daydreaming isn't just for children. It's for visionary leaders like you.

3

Walt's Communication Skills

In the spring of 1933, around the time of the release of the wildly popular Silly Symphony *The Three Little Pigs*, Walt decided to amaze the world with the first full-length animated feature, *Snow White and the Seven Dwarfs*. Long before he announced his plans to his animators, Walt began talking about the story of Snow White in meetings, in hallways, in casual conversations around the Hyperion studio. According to one early account, Walt "introduced the idea by the method of slow infiltration. He dropped it on everyone individually in the midst of casual conversations."[55]

One of the first people Walt talked to about Snow White was his boyhood friend Walter Pfeiffer, who lived in Chicago at that time.

They visited the Field Museum of Natural History together, and as they toured the exhibits, Walt told his friend the story of Snow White. He acted out the tale with such sweeping gestures and with so much emotion in his voice that a security guard thought Walt was attacking his friend—and they had to leave the museum.

Walt told the story to people around the Hyperion studio—secretaries, bookkeepers, and anyone else who would listen. He wasn't telling the bare-bones Brothers Grimm version—he was telling the Disney version, filled with action, suspense, and a dramatic conflict between innocence and evil. Each time he told the story, he would change a detail here, add more drama there, toss in a joke or two for good measure—and he would gauge his listener's reaction. He was refining the story in front of test audiences, and he was fixing the best version of the story in his mind.

After a meeting at the studio, a member of Walt's business team recalled, "Walt told us his idea of developing the story, 'Snow White,' and honestly, the way that boy can tell a story is nobody's business. I was practically in tears during some of it. . . . If it should turn out one tenth as good as the way he tells it, it should be a wow."[56]

In November 1933, Disney animator Art Babbitt wrote to his friend Bill Tytla (who was animating for Terrytoons of New Rochelle, New York), "We're definitely going ahead with a feature-length cartoon in color—they're planning the building for it now. . . . Walt has promised me a big hunk of the picture."[57] Tytla was so intrigued at the idea of a full-length animated feature that he moved to Los Angeles, joined the Disney animation staff, and became one of Walt's top animators.

In 1934, Walt gathered forty to fifty of his top animators, gave each one some cash, and told them to go have dinner, relax, and then return to the studio. "I have a story to tell you," he said. After dinner, they reconvened in a recording studio and seated themselves in a semicircle. The room was dark. Walt stood at the front of the room in the glow of a spotlight. When everyone was settled, Walt proceeded to tell them the story of Snow White. He acted out all the parts with distinct character voices, dramatic facial expressions, and grand gestures. He brought the story alive with the sheer force of his personality. The animators who were there that night didn't have to *imagine* the story of Snow White—they had *seen* it come to life before their eyes.

One animator recalled, "That one performance lasted us three years. Whenever we'd get stuck, we'd remember how Walt did it on that night."[58] Through his communication skills alone, Walt had already created the entire motion picture. All the artists had to do was animate it.

Walt was a visionary. He envisioned *Snow White and the Seven Dwarfs* in much the same way he later envisioned Disneyland. He mentally imagined every detail, rehearsed and replayed those details in his mind, then communicated it all to his staff in an emotional, unforgettable way. He understood that a vision accomplishes nothing until you communicate your vision to your people.

He also understood that communication is much more than merely speaking words. Effective communication involves a leader's entire being—facial expressions, eye contact, passion in the voice, physical gestures, and movement. Walt didn't *tell* you what he wanted you to do—he *showed* you by acting out the part.

I don't know if Walt's communication skills came naturally, if he learned them, or some combination of the two. But I know from personal experience that the art of communicating is a learnable skill. I vividly remember sweating and stammering my way through my speeches in front of Miss Barbara Bullard's ninth-grade English class. Today I make my living delivering speeches and giving media interviews. If that tongue-tied fourteen-year-old Pat Williams could learn the skill of public speaking, then believe me, *anyone* can.

Leadership requires that we communicate our vision in a powerful, persuasive, memorable way. Walt Disney communicated his vision of Snow White to his animators, and the result was one of the most beloved motion pictures of all time. He turned his visions into reality through the power of communication. To lead like Walt, we must communicate like Walt.

Walt the Salesman

Long before Walt Disney learned to draw, he was an actor.

Biographer Bob Thomas recounted an incident from Walt's boyhood involving his mother Flora. "One day Flora answered the front door," Thomas wrote, "to find a nicely dressed woman. Flora began to converse with her until she recognized some of her own clothes. The visitor was Walt in his mother's clothes, a wig and makeup."[59]

Walt also learned the art of salesmanship at an early age. When he was eighteen, he persuaded his friend, Ubbe Iwerks, to go into business with him. They formed their own company, Iwerks-Disney Commercial Artists. Walt suggested that Ubbe shorten his first name to Ub, and for the rest of his life, Iwerks went by Ub. Walt handled the cartooning and sales side of the business while Ub did more refined illustration and lettering.

Walter Pfeiffer, whose father was a union official, helped Iwerks-Disney secure its first contract, designing the United Leatherworkers' *Journal*. Walt used samples of the *Journal* as a portfolio to persuade restaurateur Al Carder, publisher of Kansas City's *Restaurant News*, to hire Iwerks-Disney. Walt offered Carder a win-win proposition: If

Carder would give Iwerks-Disney office space at no charge, he and Ub would do all of Carder's advertising art for free. Anyone that skilled in salesmanship at age eighteen is bound to go far.

I once interviewed Virginia Davis, who was the original Alice in Walt's Alice Comedies, a cartoon-and-live-action series he began while in Kansas City. She told me, "I was four when I first went to work for Walt. He was twenty-one. I just adored him. He was like a favorite uncle to me. I guess I was Walt's first star—the first Disney contract player.

"Walt was a great salesman. He could sell anything to anyone. He was also a very honest man—honest to a fault. When he gave his word, you could count on it. He was a salesman who did what he promised.

"He sold my mother on doing some of the filming for *Alice's Wonderland* in our home in Kansas City. Walt didn't have money to build sets. Instead, he brought all the lights and cameras into our home so that he could shoot the scene where my mother tucks me into bed. Later, after we finished filming *Alice's Wonderland*, Walt sold my mother on letting me go to California to make more Alice Comedies in Hollywood."

Walt succeeded because he was a salesman. Selling is an honorable profession. In one way or another, I've been a salesman throughout my adult life. I've been in the professional sports business for fifty-seven years, and I got my start as a salesman, selling advertising space in minor league baseball programs. All the wealth that has been created in the world can be traced to the act of one person selling something to somebody else.

A leader is by definition a salesperson. If you aren't selling, you aren't leading. As a leader, the first thing you have to sell is your vision. You have to communicate your vision to the people you lead with such enthusiasm, energy, and vividness that *your* vision becomes *their* vision. What does it take to be a salesperson in the Disney tradition? You need these five qualities: honesty, enthusiasm, confidence, courage, and perseverance. Let's look at each of these traits:

1. **Honesty.** Virginia Davis said that Walt was "a very honest man—honest to a fault. When he gave his word, you could count on it." All great salespeople cultivate a reputation for honesty. Yes, we all know the stereotype of the fast-talking, fly-by-night used-car salesman. But great salespeople like Walt are people of integrity. His name was his brand, and he knew that if he ever did anything to stain the Disney brand, he would never get the public to trust him again.

   Great salespeople like Walt want repeat business. He used to take his set decorator, Emile Kuri, to Disneyland once a week. (Kuri designed the interior of Walt's apartment over the Fire House and the sets of such motion pictures as *20,000 Leagues Under the Sea* and *Mary Poppins*.) Kuri recalled that he and Walt would sit on the porch of City Hall, near the Disneyland main gate, and watch people coming into the park. Somehow Walt could tell which people were visiting for the first time and which were repeat visitors—and the repeat customers always thrilled Walt. "Look," he'd say to Kuri. "They've been here before! Look at their faces, they've been here!"[60]

   Imagineer Harriet Burns told me, "Walt was a great salesman. His best sales technique was his absolute honesty. I remember many situations where we needed to sell a corporation or a financial backer on some project. When it was a crucial situation, the staff would say, 'Walt, you'll have to go.' In other words, Walt would have to go in person and sell it. And he'd do it every time. He didn't use glib talk or flashy sales methods. He simply sold his ideas with his honesty and sincerity. People could tell that he said what he meant and meant what he said. They trusted him, and that trust relationship made him a great salesman."[61]

2. **Enthusiasm.** Ollie Johnston and Frank Thomas recalled that the mid-1930s era, when Walt was gearing up to produce *Snow White*, was "easily the most thrilling period for the Disney animators."[62] The studio was growing, exploring, and experimenting. The art of animation was improving by quantum leaps. Walt had his animators studying comedic timing, staging, natural movement, exaggerated action, and the fine points of turning drawings into characters with believable personalities.

During that time, Walt hired Don Graham, the Chouinard Art Institute's top art instructor, to coach his artists in improving their drawing skills. Graham soon found that what Walt wanted his artists to achieve was not being taught in any art school in the country, including Chouinard. So Graham spent hours and hours researching and teaching himself the techniques and insights he could share with the Disney artists. Johnston and Thomas concluded, "Don soon was spending more time studying than teaching, as he tried to keep up with Walt's enthusiasm."[63]

In a 1953 profile of Walt, AP newsman Bob Thomas wrote, "One element characterizes all movies bearing the Walt Disney label. That is enthusiasm. It is not hard to account for. It comes from the head man himself."[64]

I once interviewed Disney legend Jack Lindquist, who spent almost four decades with Disney, including four years as president of Disneyland. He told me a story about Walt's contagious enthusiasm. "In 1955, before Disneyland opened," he said, "Walt attended a board meeting of the Atlantic Richfield Company (ARCO). He wanted the company to sponsor the Autopia attraction in Tomorrowland. Walt made his pitch to the board. He had artwork showing these small cars on the Autopia freeway driving past Atlantic Richfield billboards. He said, 'We'll put the Richfield name on all the billboards in the attraction.' He had them in the palm of his hand—the man could really sell.

"Walt finished his presentation, and someone asked, 'How much will it cost us to sponsor this attraction?' Walt said, 'Two hundred fifty thousand dollars—twenty-five thousand per year for ten years.' You could see the board members picking up his enthusiasm. It was very infectious.

"Finally, they asked Walt to step outside while they deliberated. A little later, they brought Walt back and said, 'We think this is a good deal for our company, and we've decided to sponsor it.' Walt said, 'Would it be possible to take the first check with me today?' And darned if they didn't go downstairs and write Walt a check for twenty-five thousand dollars on the spot. After Walt left, Leonard Firestone, one of the board members, said to the rest of the board, 'I have a question. What did we just buy?'"

Imagineer Sam McKim made a similar observation. "Walt was a salesman," McKim told me, "and he could really sell the corporate sponsors on his ideas and projects for the theme park. Executives from those big companies were fascinated by him and loved to be around him. They absorbed his enthusiasm, and their sponsorship made Disneyland possible."

3. **Confidence.** After Walt's Laugh-O-gram studio went bankrupt in 1923, he had nothing to his name but a cardboard suitcase, forty dollars in cash, and a can of film—the unfinished first episode of the Alice Comedies. He had no home, no business, and had been eating canned beans every day for weeks—yet he wrote to film distributor Margaret Winkler and confidently told her that the first Alice cartoon would be "finished very soon" and he would come to New York and present his plan for future Alice short features. Was Walt just blowing smoke? Absolutely not. He had the confident optimism of a super salesman.

In 1928, after Charles B. Mintz took Oswald the Lucky Rabbit and most of Walt's animators away from him (only Ub Iwerks, Les Clark, and Johnny Cannon remained), Walt was hurt, angry—yet amazingly confident. From New York, he wrote Roy, "I feel very confident that we will come out all right even if it is a bit disillusioning."[65]

Later, he sent Roy a telegram:

LEAVING TONIGHT STOPPING OVER KC ARRIVE HOME SUNDAY MORNING SEVEN THIRTY DON'T WORRY EVERY-THING OK WILL GIVE DETAILS WHEN ARRIVE.

Walt's wife Lillian recalled that Walt behaved like a "raging lion" on the train from New York to L.A. He was angry, yet he was also optimistic about the future and confident in his own ability to chart his own course. "All he could say, over and over," Lillian said, "was that he'd never work for anyone again as long as he lived; he'd be his own boss."[66] Great salespeople—and great leaders—are brimming with confidence, even in times of adversity. And great leaders have confidence not only in themselves but in the people they lead.

If you've ever been to a Disney theme park in Anaheim, Orlando, or anywhere else in the world, you've undoubtedly admired the statue called "Partners," depicting Walt standing hand-in-hand with Mickey Mouse. Walt's right hand points toward the horizon, as if Walt is saying, "See what we accomplished together, Mickey?" That statue was sculpted by Blaine Gibson, who said that Walt changed his life through his confident salesmanship.

"Walt had the ability to inspire us by selling us on ourselves," Gibson said. "Walt had more confidence in us as artists than we had in ourselves. I'm a sculptor now, but I used to be an animator, and I loved it. I didn't want to leave animation and go work in the theme parks. But Walt saw me as a sculptor, and he sold me on it. He made me believe I could do it. He gave us the confidence to do things we never imagined were possible."

Animator Les Clark joined the Disney studio in 1927—the first of "Disney's Nine Old Men"—the studio's core inner circle of top animators. Clark was the only artist other than Ub Iwerks to work on the original Mickey Mouse cartoons. Walt, Clark said, had "confidence in the people who worked for him, because he gave his people assignments that they didn't think they could do themselves."[67]

Confidence gives you the ability to step out of your comfort zone and tackle difficult challenges. Confidence gives you the motivation to keep selling your ideas and products even when times are tough. Confidence is an attitude you choose, not a feeling or an emotion. Even when you feel insecure and uncomfortable in a situation, you can adopt an attitude of confidence.

Nothing great was ever accomplished in a comfort zone.

Sell like Walt and lead like Walt, with an attitude of invincible confidence.

4. **Courage.** Confidence is closely linked to courage. A leader's courage builds confidence in those who follow. Every great achievement in Walt's life—the creation of Mickey Mouse, the creation of *Snow White and the Seven Dwarfs*, the creation of Disneyland—began with a courageous decision.

Harper Goff was a set designer for Warner Bros. when he chanced to meet Walt in Bassett-Lowke, Ltd., a model train shop in London in 1951. The Bassett-Lowke company sold live steam and electric locomotives. Goff wanted to purchase an antique train, but the shopkeeper told him it was reserved for another gentleman who was returning soon. When the other man entered the shop, Goff instantly recognized him as Walt Disney. Walt and Goff talked over dinner that evening, and Walt realized he had saved clippings of Goff's illustrations from *Esquire*.

Walt invited Goff to join the Disney organization. Goff served as an art director for Disney films (he designed the submarine *Nautilus* for *20,000 Leagues Under the Sea*), and also designed much of Disneyland's Main Street USA (where he often played the banjo in Ward Kimball's Dixieland band, the Firehouse Five Plus Two). Goff once told an interviewer that Walt "had the courage of his conviction, and he was the most courageous man that I've ever seen that way. Because he had courage and he had confidence in himself, he inspired confidence in people around him."[68]

Just as selling is essential to leadership, courage is the key to selling. The greatest obstacle salespeople face is the fear of rejection. If you sell anything, whether it's your vision or a product, you will experience rejection. Walt had a tough hide when it came to rejection and criticism. He never pandered to his critics and he never let rejection discourage him. He kept selling his vision and making his dreams come true.

As writer and Disney historian Craig Hodgkins observed, "Walt was completely focused on his product and his goals, not on himself. He wasn't concerned about what people thought of him. He had more important things to think about, and that's why he was so effective at selling his dreams."[69]

5. **Perseverance.** Disneyland was Walt's obsession for nearly four decades. It was on his mind the night *Snow White and the Seven Dwarfs* premiered at the Carthay Circle Theatre in 1937. As part of the promotion for the movie, Disney artists had created a life-sized diorama called Dwarfland on Wilshire Boulevard, a short walk from the theater. It featured a dwarf-sized cottage that children could walk through, three-foot-tall mushrooms painted in different colors, spooky trees with grasping limbs and evil-looking eyes, a water wheel mill with a waterfall, and the Seven Dwarfs' diamond mine.

Animator Wilfred Jackson stood beside Walt as he inspected the diorama. "Someday," Walt said, "I want to build a park for kids to play in—a place with fantasy cottages like these, all scaled down to a child's size."

By that time, Walt had been dreaming of building such a place for some twenty years, and it would be eighteen more years before Disneyland would open its gates to welcome the world. To achieve his vision, Walt had to communicate that vision again and again, to bankers, television executives, sponsors,

Imagineers, and above all, his own brother, Roy O. Disney. Walt might have been the greatest salesman in the world, but Roy displayed the toughest sales resistance in the world. Walt had to pitch his Disneyland vision to Roy again and again. If not for Walt's perseverance as a salesman and a visionary communicator, none of the Disney theme parks would exist today.

Walt's biographer, journalist Bob Thomas, told me, "Walt succeeded because he was persistent and determined. He didn't let rejection and criticism stop him. He didn't listen to the naysayers who told him he couldn't do this or that. Walt was a finisher."

You can't stop great salespeople. They are obsessed with their vision, and they keep smiling, pitching, selling, and persevering. They can't even hear the naysayers. They pay rejection no heed. They keep selling their dreams until the dream becomes a reality.

Walt's Communication Skills

Walt told Bob Thomas, "I was stumped one day when a little boy asked, 'Do you draw Mickey Mouse?' And I had to admit I do not draw anymore. 'Then you think up all the jokes and ideas?' 'No,' I said, I don't do that.' Finally, he looked at me and said, 'Mr. Disney, just what do you do?' 'Well,' I said, 'sometimes I think of myself as a little bee. I go from one area of the studio to another, and I gather pollen and sort of stimulate everybody. I guess that's the job I do.'"[70]

Walt was describing how he led by communicating. He had the big picture in his mind, the vision for every project his studio was producing. He would visit the story artists, the background artists, the animators, and the musical directors, and he would gather the "pollen" of ideas and inspiration—then he would spread that "pollen" throughout the studio, wherever it was needed. Walt was a great leader because he was a skilled communicator. He communicated simply and directly, and when he talked, people listened—and they responded. He persuaded, he motivated, and he energized people to turn his vision into a reality.

Disney composer Richard Sherman told me, "Walt had a way of communicating that was just magical. Simple, but magical. He would give you a challenge and say, 'I know you can do this.' He made you believe anything was possible. He made you proud to be on his team. He saw potential in people who had never really done anything great. My brother Robert and I really had no track record in the music industry, but Walt heard a few of our songs and he gave us an opportunity and inspired us to keep topping ourselves. Without Walt to inspire us, I don't know where we'd be today."

What made Walt such an inspiring communicator? "He always wanted you to find something wonderful in yourself," Richard said. "He wanted you to find something to believe in—God's gift to you. God gives you the gift, and the rest is up to you. Walt taught me that what you do with that gift is your gift back to God."

Walt had a reputation for setting high standards and being demanding—yet the Sherman brothers found him to be understanding and affirming. "Walt would never condemn you," Richard told me. "If you failed, he'd just steer you in a new direction. At Disney, I attended the most inspiring graduate school in the world. I learned something from Walt every day."

Communication is far more than the words we speak. Walt understood that people are designed to send and receive messages through eye contact, facial expressions, smiles, frowns, hand gestures, movement, and posture. He had studied Charlie Chaplin, an actor in the silent movie era who communicated meaning and emotion through his facial expression, gestures, and eyes. Walt had learned nonverbal communication from the master of the art form. That's why he communicated so effectively, whether as a performer before a mass audience or in one-on-one conversations.

Actress Margaret Kerry recalled that one of Walt's great strengths as a communicator was his gift of storytelling. She told me, "When I was working as a reference model for Tinker Bell in *Peter Pan*, Walt could act out the whole story himself. Then he could show you how your part fit together with every other part of the story. When he was telling you a story, he had your complete attention."

Walt's communication skills were especially important in his relationship with reporters. Bob Thomas recalled that his interviews with Walt during the 1950s and 1960s followed a specific ritual. "The procedure was always the same," he wrote. "The reporter went at noon with Disney's public relations man to the award-decorated office on the third floor of the animation building. A secretary served tomato juice to Walt and the visitors, and Walt began talking." (The "tomato juice" was probably V8 juice, Walt's favorite.)

There was no desk in Walt's office, just a low table stacked with reports and scripts. The office walls were lined with mementos, plaques, awards, and ceramic figurines of Mickey, Snow White, the Dwarfs, and other Disney characters. On the wall opposite the table were two framed exhibits: a blowup of the *Variety* list of all-time box-office leaders with *Mary Poppins* at number four (behind *Gone with the Wind*, *Ben-Hur*, and *The Ten Commandments*) and an aerial map of Disneyland showing additions Walt was planning for the future.

Walt would usually talk for a while about projects he had planned for the next four or five years, then he'd say, "Let's go eat." And Walt would walk the reporter down Dopey Drive to the studio commissary. "Along the way," Thomas wrote, "he said hello to the employees; virtually all called him 'Walt,' but the casualness was not to be mistaken for intimacy. There was always a respectful distance between employees and the boss."

In the commissary, Walt and his guests would sit at the corner table in the Coral Room, the executive dining room. Walt would always order light fare ("he was usually on a diet to lose a few pounds," Thomas added), then resume the conversation. "Like many men of vast creativity," the reporter added, "Walt was impatient with the usual give-and-take of a press interview. He would grasp a thought, examine it, expand it, and pursue it to the extreme."

Thomas recalled a time during one interview when Walt described the antics of Baloo the Bear in *The Jungle Book*: "His eyebrows would waggle and his cheeks would puff up bear-like; he was as good a storyteller in person as he was on the screen."

Bob Thomas had many such lunchtime meetings with Walt over the twenty-plus years of their acquaintance, and he also accompanied Walt on a number of visits to Disneyland. "He talked of things present and future, and often relived events of his past. He revealed himself as a creator of fantasies, but...he drew the line on any invasion of his personal life."[71]

Walt and Television

Walt was the first movie mogul to recognize the power and influence of television. In May 1939, a few days before the Disney cartoon "Donald's Cousin Gus" debuted in theaters, Walt permitted NBC's experimental TV station in Manhattan to broadcast the cartoon to a few TV sets around the city. In October of that year, Walt sent a memo to Roy and the studio's legal department, stating, "Everything we do in the future should include television rights. There might be a big angle of television for the shows we have already produced."[72]

"Walt had the voice of a prophet," Disney story artist Joe Grant said. "I remember the time when television was on its way in and I said to Walt, 'Why aren't we on TV?' He said, 'Television will come to us,' and it did. He knew ahead of time."[73]

And television did come to Walt. All the major networks wanted Walt to produce content for their airwaves. In 1950, Walt hired a research company, C. J. LaRoche, to perform a risk/benefit report titled *Television for Walt Disney Productions*. The report was completed in September. Soon afterward, the Disney Studio announced it would produce a Christmas special to promote the release of *Alice in Wonderland*.

The first Disney TV special, *One Hour in Wonderland*, aired on NBC at 4 PM, Christmas Day 1950, sponsored by Coca-Cola. Along with Walt, the show featured ventriloquist Edgar Bergen, his wooden costars Charlie McCarthy and Mortimer Snerd, actress Kathryn Beaumont (the voice of Alice), and Walt's daughters, Diane and Sharon. Though there were only 10.5 million TV sets in America at that time, the show was watched by 20 million viewers. The following year, a second Disney special, *The Walt Disney Christmas Show*, was broadcast on CBS at 3 PM on Christmas Day.[74]

The Disney Christmas shows marked a major transition for the Disney studio. No longer was Disney merely a motion picture studio. It was on the way to becoming a multimedia empire. Walt later said, "Instead of considering television a rival...I said, 'I can use that.'

Television is an 'open sesame' to many things. I don't have to worry about going out and selling the theater man....I go directly to my public."[75]

The *Disneyland* television series premiered on ABC in October 1954. The Davy Crockett episodes touched off a nationwide craze, with soaring sales of 45 rpm recordings of "The Ballad of Davy Crockett" and Crockett-style coonskin caps. Not only did the *Disneyland* show sell movie tickets and merchandise, but it also communicated a positive message for the next generation.

Walt told Bob Thomas, "One of the things I want to do is make a picture that shows the good side of teenagers. I get so put out with all these pictures about delinquency. I thought that one about Marlon Brando and the motorcycles was bad [referring to *The Wild One*], and *The Blackboard Jungle* upset me for three days afterward. I think those pictures are a mistake.... Kids get bad ideas when they see such things on the screen.

"And I don't think they show a true picture of young people today. All in all, I think kids are a good bunch. There are some bad ones, but there always have been. I remember when I was a kid in Kansas City, a bunch of kids were breaking into houses and storing the loot in the cellar of an unfinished church."

Walt also believed it was a mistake to lecture young people. "I don't want anything that preaches to kids about how to be good," he said. "I've had them take such things out of the *Mickey Mouse Club*, too, except for little things like 'words to grow by.' Preaching won't keep kids out of trouble. But keeping their minds occupied will."

The best way to keep kids out of trouble, he said, was to inspire them with a fascination for the world around them. He produced many documentary films that were shown in public schools, such as *Our Friend the Atom*, as well as the "science-factual" episodes of his *Disneyland* TV series ("Man in Space" and "Mars and Beyond").

"I think we can do a lot more things like the atom and space features," Walt said. "I'd like to tackle a subject like mathematics and try to make it interesting to young people."[76] (In 1959, Disney released *Donald in Mathmagic Land*, a half-hour educational film widely distributed in schools and nominated for an Academy Award.)

Walt hosted the *Disneyland* TV series for thirteen seasons (the title was changed to *Walt Disney Presents* in 1958, then to *Walt Disney's Wonderful World of Color* when the show moved from ABC to NBC in 1961). Walt's warm and genial personality soon earned him the nickname "Uncle Walt." Though Walt was initially insecure in the role of television host, he quickly took to it. The role fit him like a comfortable shoe.

He filmed most of his host introductions on a set at the Disney studio in Burbank. The set was a replica of Walt's third-floor office in the Animation Building, and he looked at ease and at home in front of the cameras. He would usually film introductions for multiple shows in one day (sometimes a dozen or more in a three-day period).

The first producer for the *Disneyland* series, Bill Walsh, recalled, "Once he began performing every week, he kind of liked it. It uncovered a streak of ham in him." Another producer on the Disney anthology series, Winston Hibler, said, "In the early days, Walt would help write his own dialogue. He never liked stilted dialogue or anything that was too formalized. He said, 'I like to talk the way that people talk.'"[77] That's an important insight. The most effective communication is simple, informal talk—no oratory, just a lively, friendly conversation with the viewer.

Walt also liked to use props and costumes to make an impression on his audience—and on network executives. In the 1950s, TV programming was dominated by Westerns, such as *Wagon Train, The Lone Ranger, Wyatt Earp,* and *Gunsmoke.* ABC execs pressured Walt to feature Westerns on *Disneyland*—but Walt was a trend-setter, not a trend-follower. He would only produce Westerns if he could make them on his own terms.

Donn Tatum, an ABC executive in the 1950s who later became president of Walt Disney Productions, recalled, "We had a meeting set up and in came Walt wearing a cowboy outfit and two guns. He threw the guns on the table and said, 'Okay, you want Westerns, you're gonna have Westerns.' He proceeded to recount the whole story of Texas John Slaughter, and then the story of Elfego Baca, a self-appointed sheriff in old New Mexico. The network executives' eyes were all bugging out and Walt said, 'We're gonna give you the *true* heroes and the *true* West!'"[78] And when Walt introduced those Westerns as the host of *Disneyland,* he was wearing that same cowboy outfit and guns.

Walt was a wizard of communication, and his effect on his audience was sheer magic. Disney historian Jim Korkis recalled Walt's impact as a communicator: "When each week, off-camera announcer Dick Wesson in his distinctive voice said, 'And, now your host … Walt Disney,' it was as if Ali Baba had uttered the words 'Open Sesame' and a cave of sparkling treasures was suddenly unveiled."[79]

What can we learn about the leadership skill of communication from Walt's example? Here are the lessons I've learned:

1. **Become a salesperson.** To lead like Walt, learn to sell like Walt. Sell your vision, your ideas, your confidence, your leadership. Build a reputation for integrity and trustworthiness, so that you can sell your ideas to the same people again and again. Remember, if you aren't selling, you aren't leading.

2. **Become an actor.** To communicate like Walt, with power and persuasion, become an actor. Communicate not just with your words, but with your eyes, your face, your arms, your whole body. Get into the part, feel it and believe it, then sell it to your listeners.

3. **Guard your integrity.** Cultivate a reputation for absolute honesty, then sell your vision, sell your organization, and sell your leadership ability. Sell with enthusiasm, energy, and conviction—but above all, sell with integrity.

   Any huckster can make a one-time sale to one customer. But the key to repeat business is *trust*, built on a foundation of integrity. A great salesperson underpromises and overdelivers. If you are known for your honesty, you'll always have loyal customers and you'll always be successful as a salesperson.

4. **Communicate your enthusiasm.** Enthusiasm is contagious. Enthusiasm persuades. Enthusiasm motivates. All great salespeople are fired up with enthusiasm for their product. All great leaders are brimming with enthusiasm about their vision.

5. **Communicate your optimism.** Talk to the people you lead, both in mass settings and one-on-one. Encourage them and tell them you believe in them. Communicate confidence. Communicate courage. Communicate the will to persevere in the face of criticism or adversity.

   Have you lost your own Oswald the Lucky Rabbit? Don't lose your positive attitude. You've got what it takes to think up your own Mickey Mouse, your own winning idea. When Walt lost Oswald, he wrote to Roy, "I feel very confident that we will come out all right," and he telegrammed DON'T WORRY EVERYTHING OK.

To lead like Walt, communicate your optimism to everyone around you. Demonstrate confidence in yourself and your people. Inspire your people with hope and a can-do attitude. If you communicate courage in times of crisis, you will inspire loyalty and perseverance in the people you lead.

6. **Become a storyteller.** Stories don't just grab your listeners' attention—stories grab their *emotions*. Stories instruct and make your message unforgettable. People may forget your brilliant three-point outline, but they'll remember your stories, and they'll never forget the lessons those stories taught them. Tell your stories the way Walt told them—vividly, with energy and expression, with gestures and action, with emotion and eye communication. Make your stories come alive in the imagination of your listeners.

Walt led by communicating. He made *Snow White and the Seven Dwarfs* by communicating his vision to his artists. He built Disneyland by communicating his vision to television audiences. What is your vision? How will you make your dreams come true as Walt did? Lead by communicating—then go build some castles and kingdoms of your own.

4

Walt's People Skills

In 1920, nineteen-year-old Walt Disney took a job at the Kansas City Film Ad Company. At his previous place of employment, the Pesmen-Rubin Commercial Art Studio, there was no time clock to punch. So he was dismayed to learn that his new employer required all employees to punch in and punch out. Viewing the time clock as an insult to his dignity as an artist, Walt refused to comply.

He completely ignored the time clock during his first two days on the job. On the third day, the company timekeeper came to Walt and said, "What's the big idea?"

Walt told the man that time clocks are dehumanizing. He refused to use them. He would arrive on time, and leave when his work was done, but he was not going to punch a time clock.

The timekeeper warned Walt that if he didn't want to be unemployed, he'd better punch his time card. But Walt was adamant. He told the timekeeper, even if it cost him his job, he refused to be a slave to a time clock.

The timekeeper waited until the end of Walt's first week on the job, then he took Walt's blank time cards to the head of the company. The boss summoned Walt to his office. Walt arrived, expecting to be fired on the spot. Instead, he found the boss surprisingly sympathetic.

"Walter, I can understand your point of view," the man said. "But what you're doing is bad for morale. Can't you see that?"

The boss's appeal to company morale made sense to Walt. The timekeeper had simply demanded that Walt knuckle under to company policy, which made Walt feel demeaned. But the boss had explained the situation in terms of respect for the feelings and morale of his coworkers. Walt agreed to comply with the policy.[80]

When Walt founded his own studio—first in Kansas City, then on Kingswell Avenue in Los Angeles, then on Hyperion Street, and finally in Burbank—he steadfastly refused to install a time clock. He would not impose a burden on his employees that he had hated when he was a young artist at the Kansas City Film Ad Company. He wanted the studio to feel like a family, not a factory.

Story artist Carl Barks recalled the friendly, open atmosphere in the early days of the Burbank studio. "The Disney studios were a place where there were no time clocks," he said. "We were able to come to work whenever we wanted to. If you went to work, did a good job and had something to show for your efforts, you got paid damn well."[81]

In addition to his no-time-clock policy, Walt maintained a generous sick leave policy at the Hyperion studio and during the early days at the Burbank studio. Anyone could take three sick days in a week with full pay, no questions asked. Longer paid sick leaves were granted with a doctor's note. Walt would also close the studio for two weeks in late August or early September to give the entire staff a paid vacation. As an item in the *Oakland Tribune* (September 14, 1932) noted, "Ben Sharpsteen, once an artist on this paper and now a Mickey Mouse cartoonist, dropped in last week on a visit. Walt Disney closed down the studio for two weeks to give vacations to all hands."[82]

Unfortunately, Walt's no-time-clock policy and other generous perks were killed by the bitter animators' strike of 1941. "I was against the strike," Carl Barks recalled. "I had the feeling that something was being destroyed.... It was these shirkers and complainers who had organized this strike. Disney was fair—of course, he could have been more considerate and humane to his employees, but those were hard times."[83]

On August 11, 1941, as the strike dragged on, Walt, Lillian, and fifteen Disney employees flew out of Burbank for a three-month South American goodwill tour. In Walt's absence, Roy and legal counsel Gunther Lessing dealt with the union and federal arbitrators. When the strike officially ended and animators returned to work in mid-September, they found that the studio had installed time clocks.[84]

When Walt returned from Latin America, he permitted the time clocks to remain—a tangible symbol of the shattered trust between Walt and his staff. The strike had estranged Walt from his animators, and he saw no point in treating his artists like family if they were going to treat him like the enemy.

Walt had always thought of his studio as a creative community, even a family. With a sense of paternal pride and fondness, he had called his artists "my boys." From his earliest years as head of the

Disney studio, he had tried to create an environment that was fun, relaxed, and considerate of the needs of his employees.

The strike was a sad turning point in Walt's leadership career.

Knowing People as Individuals

Imagineer Rolly Crump, who joined the studio in 1952, said that Walt connected differently with each person at the studio. Walt made an effort to know each one as an individual—and by knowing them so well, he inspired them to reach undreamed-of heights of achievement. Rolly concluded:

> Walt was able to reach inside you and bring to the surface a part of you that even you didn't know existed. He brought out the best in the people around him.
>
> He brought out the best in me.[85]

In October 2018, my friend Peggy Matthews Rose attended an event where Walt's master vehicle designer Bob Gurr spoke about Walt's ability to bring out the best in people—including Bob's friend, the wildly creative Imagineer Rolly Crump. Peggy shared some of Bob Gurr's insights with me.

When someone in the audience asked Bob what Disneyland needs more of today, Bob replied, "It needs more of the kind of pixie dust that Rolly Crump was able to produce right under Walt's nose." Bob noted that Walt could be stern with people who needed a tougher approach, but Rolly was a special case.

"Walt tolerated Rolly," Bob said. Rolly Crump was not a "yes-man," and Walt seemed to appreciate Rolly's directness and candor. "Rolly always had an opinion," Bob added, "and whether you asked him for it or not, you got it anyway. And his opinion was not necessarily for publication—but everybody understood that if Rolly said, 'It's good,' it's good. I'd like to see more of that kind of honesty and more pixie-like, charming creations like Rolly made for the Enchanted Tiki Room."

Bob said that Disneyland operates today with a conventional top-down business management model, with the CEO at the top and layers of MBAs below. When a leader in the company wants to know why something's not working at a lower level, the leader sends a memo or email down through the chain of command. Weeks or months later, an answer filters back up to the leader, who says, "That's not right. That's not what I want." Then the leader sends another memo or email, and on and on it goes.

That's not how Walt got things done. Gurr said, "Walt would get up out of his chair, leave his office, and wander around, particularly the shops—the model shop, the machine shop at the studio. If there was something he wanted to see, if he wanted to make sure a project was working all right, he'd go down and look at it in person."

Bob Gurr recalled that Walt had a special way of conveying his wishes and giving direction without stifling an employee's creativity. He wouldn't say, "That's all wrong—that's not what I told you to do!" Instead, Walt would look at a person's work and say, "I have another idea that I think might work well. Would you give some thought to this?"

"Guess what Walt just did," Gurr said. "He has engaged you to improve something of yours that wasn't very good—yet he never told you it wasn't any good! Think of that! He's hired you, he knows you're a creative person, and he's making sure you feel free to create without any feelings of recrimination. Walt doesn't want to intimidate you. He doesn't want to scare you so that you'll be afraid to speak up whenever he comes around. He'd never give an order. He'd always ask a question. And he'd leave you free to use your own creativity.

"Walt would come to me and say, 'Bobby, we're getting started on something and I'd like you to get going on it right away.' And then he'd walk away and let me get started. A week later, he'd come by and say, 'Yeah, that's kind of interesting. But what if—?' And he'd suggest this new thing he wanted to add. That was Walt's secret weapon. He was never intimidating. He was always asking questions to ignite your creativity. And when he's got a creative guy like Rolly Crump who's ready to jump up with an idea or a sketch at any moment, Walt's approach really works. That's why we have the Tiki Room and 'it's a small world.'"[86]

Longtime cast member Earl Williams began his Disneyland career in 1964. One of his early jobs was maintaining the Jungle Cruise attraction, which included cleaning leaves out of the traps that filtered the river water. One night, he was working down by the Jungle Cruise boats when he saw Walt on the walkway behind the Carnation Café, walking toward his Fire House apartment. It was the first time Earl had ever seen Walt in person.

"Good evening, Mr. Disney," Earl called out.

Walt walked over to him and asked his name.

"I'm Earl," he said.

"Hi, Earl. You know, around here, we're all family and we go by our first names. And my name is Walt. So the next time you see me, you just say, 'Hi, Walt.'"

Three days later, Earl was again down by the Jungle Cruise boats and he saw Walt on his way to his apartment. He called out, "Hi, Walt!"

And Walt replied, "Hi, Earl!"

Recalling that encounter, Earl Williams said, "I have never forgotten that." He went on to work at Disneyland for forty years.[87]

Getting to know your people by name and treating them as individuals is one of the most important skills a leader can have. These are people skills that anyone can learn and that every leader should possess.

The Beverage of Conversation

Walt loved coffee. His wife Lillian once said, "Walt ate very simply. Lunch was usually just a sandwich, milk, and coffee. He always wanted coffee for lunch."[88] To Walt, coffee was the beverage of conversation. A steaming cup of coffee always set the tone for a relaxed conversation. Sharing coffee was one of the ways Walt demonstrated his people skills and got to know his employees.

Disney sound engineer Gary Carlson told me, "One day in late 1965, I was working in my office and Walt knocked on the door. He was carrying two cups of coffee, and he gave one to me and sat down. We spent the next two and a half hours just talking. He told me about his life and asked me about mine. We talked about all kinds of things. I wish I'd had a tape recorder. Walt was just a warm, friendly, regular guy. Of course, you always knew he was the boss, but he was not some towering, intimidating boss. He was very approachable."

Dick May was a World War II veteran and a teacher and counselor in the Anaheim public schools. Beginning in 1956, he also worked part-time as a Disneyland cast member. May told David Koenig and Craig Hodgkins that when Walt spent the night in his apartment over the Fire House, he would often brew a pot of coffee then stroll down Main Street with the coffee pot and some disposable cups. Sometimes wearing a bathrobe and slippers, he'd engage the night-shift cleaning crew in conversation, asking questions, giving encouragement and affirmation, and telling them about his plans for the park.[89]

Renie Bardeau, Disneyland's longtime chief photographer, had a favorite story about Walt—and again, it centered around coffee. One Saturday morning, about a half hour before Disneyland opened, Bardeau was sitting in the patio of the Hills Brothers Coffee Garden (which became the Town Square Café in 1976 and closed in 1992). Bardeau was relaxing with a cup of coffee and the morning paper when Walt came in and joined him.

A waitress appeared, recognized Walt, and became so nervous that her voice quavered and her hands shook. "Is there anything I can get for you, Mr. Disney?" she said.

Walt sought to calm her jitters. "Call me Walt," he said gently. "There are only two 'misters' in Disneyland, Mr. Lincoln and Mr. Toad."

The waitress, still visibly nervous, brought Walt a cup of coffee and Walt sat and talked with Bardeau about Disneyland, asking his opinion on several matters. When it came time for the park to open for business, Walt excused himself and disappeared backstage.

"He was very easy to talk to," Bardeau said of Walt. "He loved Disneyland and loved to talk to you about the park, asking you what you thought of it."[90]

One of Walt's greatest people skills was his ability to engage people in conversation, his knack for drawing out their ideas and opinions and reactions. From his early days as head of the Disney Brothers Studio to the end of his life, Walt cultivated a culture of informality. He insisted that people call him Walt, and he corrected anyone who called him "Mr. Disney" or "sir." He understood that conversations are more candid in a relaxed and informal atmosphere.

And nothing promotes a relaxed conversation like a cup of hot coffee.

Walt and His Fans

One Sunday morning in the late 1950s, Walt was walking in Frontierland with Herb Ryman, the artist who drew the first map of Disneyland. As they walked, Walt described his plans for a new themed land that would be carved out of Frontierland—a place Walt called New Orleans Square. Attendance at the park was light that morning, so Walt was able to stroll through Frontierland without being mobbed.

As Walt pointed here and there, describing his vision for New Orleans Square, Ryman noticed four women approaching. One of the women touched Walt's shoulder and said in an awed voice, "Pardon me, but you're Walt Disney."

Ryman expected Walt to be annoyed. Instead, he flashed a warm smile, shaking hands with each lady. "How are you?" he said as if he had known them all his life.

The spokeswoman blushed and said, "Oh, you don't know me."

"I do now."

She asked if Walt would sign their autograph books.

"I'd be delighted." Walt signed autographs for each lady and they walked away completely charmed. He had ensured that this would be a day they'd talk about for years.[91]

In the late 1950s, Dick May worked in the ticket booth at the Casey Jr. Circus Train. A woman in line stepped up to the window and asked, "Does Mr. Disney ever come around here?"

Before May could reply, Walt stepped up behind her and said, "Yes, I do." As was his custom, he'd been waiting in line, listening and observing while going unnoticed. The woman had been standing next to Walt without realizing it. Walt proceeded to ask for her impressions of his park.

On another occasion, Dick May was testing the new and improved Skyway between Fantasyland and Tomorrowland. Walt approached and asked May how the new Skyway cabins compared with the older version.

May said that the new version was much better and the line of people now moved faster. Walt was glad to hear it. "That's why we spent the extra money," he said—then he was gone.

"Most of the time," May recalled, "he would walk through the park alone—no security or anyone with him—with his hands in his pockets and his hat brim pulled down low. It was his way of getting a feel for how people were reacting to his park and finding out what could be done to improve the show."

Cast members who worked on Main Street always had advance notice that Walt was in the park. On their way to Main Street, they would pass the rear of the Fire House. If Walt was on the property, his big gray Lincoln would be parked backstage, near the Fire House stairs.

Dick May recalled that Walt would be very patient and charitable, even when guests were rude. One day, May was on Tom Sawyer Island, in charge of the Tom Sawyer Island Rafts. He saw Walt walking on the island, making one of his inspection tours. A man recognized Walt and roughly grabbed him by the arm, pulling him to where his wife and child waited. "Walt," the man said, "I want my kid to meet you."

Ignoring the manhandling he had just received from a guest, Walt knelt in front of the little boy and turned on the charm. He asked the boy's name, where he came from, his favorite ride, and on and on. Walt's people skills, especially in relating to his guests, were unmatched. Walt turned a potentially tense moment into an unforgettable day at Disneyland.[92]

Bob Gurr worked with Walt for twelve years, designing vehicles for Disneyland attractions. To Bob, Walt was "about as open and ordinary as anybody you'd ever run across." So he found it fascinating to be with Walt when corporate executives met him and were star-struck in his presence.

Gurr recalled a business meeting with Walt and other Disney executives at the Westinghouse Electric Corporation headquarters in Pittsburgh. After the meeting, there was a party in a bar, and Westinghouse CEO Don Burnham was talking to Walt. Burnham was so nervous in Walt's presence that his lower lip quivered. That was when Gurr realized that people out in the world—including high-powered executives—viewed Walt differently than he did. To them, Walt was a living legend, the creator of Mickey Mouse and Snow White and Disneyland.

From then on, Bob Gurr paid close attention to the people skills Walt used to climb down from the pedestal people put him on. "In order for Walt to have a conversation with somebody," Gurr said, "he's got to be able to have everybody at the same level. And I would see him deliberately loosen his tie and leave it slightly askew. Or sometimes we'd be someplace where he was wearing a little hat. He had a porkpie hat; he'd just wad up in his pocket.... He'd flop it on his head and not even readjust it. Just wherever it hit, it hit."[93] Why? Because Walt was sending a subliminal message: *Don't be nervous around me. I'm just a regular guy.*

Many celebrities revel in the hero-worship of their fans. Walt didn't want worship. He wanted conversations with people. He wanted to close the distance between himself and other people. So he invented techniques for making himself more approachable.

The People Skill of Spotting Talent

Salvador "Tutti" Camarata was a composer, arranger, and record producer. He studied music at Juilliard and played trumpet with the Jimmy and Tommy Dorsey and Benny Goodman bands. He also produced classical recordings for London Records. In 1956, Walt hired him to form Disneyland Records and serve as the music director for the label (now called Walt Disney Records). He told me, "Walt challenged and inspired you by talking to you. He wouldn't give you detailed instructions. Instead, he'd simply point you in the direction he wanted you to go, then leave the rest up to you. He'd get you started on the creative process and inspire you with confidence. As a result, you would go far beyond what you thought you were capable of doing."

In 1950, while TV was in its infancy, Walt decided to produce a Christmas television special for NBC. He tapped Bill Walsh, the scriptwriter for the Mickey Mouse daily newspaper comics, to write and produce the show. Walsh protested, "I don't have any experience in TV!" Walt replied, "Who does?"[94]

Walsh's first outing as a television writer-producer was a huge success. The following year, he produced Disney's second holiday special, *The Walt Disney Christmas Show*, which aired on CBS—another big success. Just like that, Bill Walsh was a television producer. He went on to produce the *Disneyland* TV series that premiered on ABC on Wednesday, October 27, 1954.

After the *Disneyland* series was up and running, Walt approached Bill Walsh and said, "I'm taking you off the weekly TV show and I'm going to put you on a new show. It's called *The Mickey Mouse Club*, and it's an hour-long show, five days a week."[95]

Walsh groaned. Walt had just multiplied his workload by five.

Still, Walsh succeeded as the producer of the new series, and he soon graduated to writing and producing a string of hit Disney live-action feature films, including *The Absent-Minded Professor*, *Son of Flubber*, *The Misadventures of Merlin Jones*, *That Darn Cat!*, and *Mary Poppins* (which earned Walsh two Academy Award nominations: Best Picture and Best Writing).

X Atencio was one of Walt's most amazing talent discoveries. Born Francis Xavier Atencio, X began his Disney career in 1938, signing on as an apprentice animator. He spent nearly three decades in feature animation, and his work appeared in such Disney classics as *Pinocchio* and *Dumbo*.

"I was an animator all those years," X told me. "One day Walt said, 'X, it's time for you to move.' He sent me over to the WED Enterprises, where they were building attractions for Disneyland. When I got there, I said, 'Walt sent me. What do you want me to do?' And nobody had a clue what I was supposed to do there. Walt hadn't told anyone. And I was there for a few days without any work to do.

"Finally, Walt called and said, 'X, I want you to write the script for the Pirates of the Caribbean attraction. There will be scenes with pirates and townspeople and so forth, and I want you to write the dialogue.' I wondered if Walt was talking to the right guy. I had never scripted anything before, but Walt said, 'I know you can do this.' And that's how I became a writer."

So X went to work, doing something he had never done before. He produced a script and showed it to Walt. "That's fine," Walt said. "Keep going."

"I think we should have a song playing throughout the attraction," X said. "Something like this." He sang a few bars of "Yo Ho, Yo Ho, a Pirate's Life for Me."

"Oh, this is good," Walt said, adding that if he needed any musical help, Disney composer George Bruns could assist him.

Pirates of the Caribbean opened in 1967 and instantly became one of the most popular attractions at Disneyland, in large part because of X's script and original song. X went on to write the script and songs for Disneyland's Haunted Mansion, which opened in 1969. More than fifty years later, these are still two of the most popular attractions in Disneyland—tangible proof that Walt knew what he was doing when he turned an animator named X into a scriptwriter and songwriter.

On August 14, 1954, an item appeared on the TV-Radio page of the *Los Angeles Times*, headlined "Unknown Gets Disney Role in TV Film." It read:

> Fess Parker, a comparatively unknown actor, yesterday was signed by Walt Disney for the title role of Davy Crockett in the folklore trilogy to be shown on the *Disneyland* TV series Oct. 27.
>
> One of the items that tossed the choice Parker's way is his striking physical resemblance to the pioneer patriot. He's 6 feet 5 inches tall, weighs 210 pounds, has green eyes, brown hair and an authentic backwoods drawl.[96]

The humble and self-effacing Fess Parker told an interviewer in 1955, "I reckon I'm just about the most fortunate person in all of show business." Born in Fort Worth, Fess Parker served in the Navy in World War II. After the war, he resumed his education. He was on the campus of the University of Texas in Austin when actor Adolphe Menjou came to narrate a performance of Sergei Prokofiev's *Peter and the Wolf*. Menjou spotted Parker and told him he should try acting. Parker had never given a thought to show business, but Menjou persuaded him to try.

Parker arrived in Hollywood in 1949 and enrolled in a theater class at the University of Southern California. There he was recruited for a small role in a stage production of Joshua Logan's *Mister Roberts*. He sometimes hitchhiked between L.A. and San Francisco and was once picked up by film director Walter Huston. His conversation with Huston deepened his passion for acting.

In Hollywood, however, he met a solid wall of rejection. Agents told him he didn't have what it takes. Natasha Lytess, Marilyn Monroe's acting coach, refused him, calling him "practically uncoachable." He landed bit parts in a few films, including *Them!*, a 1954 science fiction shocker about giant mutant ants. Walt screened the film while scouting its star, James Arness, for the Crockett role. But when Walt spotted Fess Parker's brief appearance as an airplane pilot who had seen giant ants in the sky, he knew he'd found his "King of the Wild Frontier."[97]

I once interviewed Fess Parker and he told me, "Walt happened to spot me in a role so small that if you looked away to put cream in your coffee, you'd miss me altogether. Walt said, 'Who's that fella?' Nobody knew. So Tom Blackburn, one of Walt's producers, got ahold of Warner Brothers and got my name. They called me out to the studio for an interview."

Fess Parker was twenty-nine when Walt Disney tested him for the role at the Burbank studio. "I brought my little guitar with me, even though I wasn't much of a singer. After Walt and I talked for a while, he said, 'Why don't you play me a little tune?' I had written a song called 'Lonely,' about a guy who had broken up with his girl and was riding on a train. I did the sound of a train whistle in the song. I later found out that Walt's other passion in life was railroads. I suppose that didn't hurt my chances.

"Walt spotted me, yanked me out of obscurity, and opened every door in the world to me. He was awfully happy with the success of *Davy Crockett*, but no happier than I was. I'll always be grateful to Walt. He gave me something in life no one else could have given me."

A Collector of People and Builder of Teams

When Walt was planning Disneyland and visiting amusement parks, he met George Whitney Jr., whose father co-owned San Francisco's Playland on the Beach. Walt hired George Whitney, Jr. to help him build Disneyland. Whitney was Disneyland employee number seven, and he served as the director of ride operations from 1954 to 1958. He is credited with mapping out the best locations of attraction entrances and exits to improve traffic flow. When his father died in 1958, Whitney returned to San Francisco to manage Playland on the Beach, yet his early contributions to Disneyland were not forgotten. His name is on a window above the Market House on Main Street.

Disneyland's first vehicle designer, Bob Gurr, called Walt "a collector of people." Walt had the ability to recognize and unlock hidden potential in people. But how did he do it? How did he know that the writer of the Mickey Mouse comic strip could become a TV producer? How did he know that an animator named X could write scripts and songs? How did Walt know that a bit player in a movie about giant ants could become a star?

Some have said Walt's ability to spot talent was a "gift" or a "knack." I disagree. I think it was a skill Walt consciously developed. We can't acquire a "knack," but we can learn a skill. What did Walt do differently from other leaders that made him such an effective judge of talent?

Let me suggest four approaches Walt used to spot hidden talent in his organization:

1. **Walt refused to pigeonhole people.** He didn't believe people were defined by a job description. He believed a person who is creative as an animator might also be creative as a storyteller, a musician, a sculptor, or an Imagineer.

   When Walt decided to make *Mary Poppins* as a musical, he put the music first, placing the project in the hands of his composers, Richard Sherman and Robert Sherman. He gave them a copy of P. L. Travers' original book and told them to find the filmable story in it. The Sherman brothers read the book, then went to the table of contents and circled six of the book's twelve chapters. When they showed that page to Walt, he opened his own copy of the book. He had circled the same six chapters.

   Walt teamed the Sherman brothers with story artist Don DaGradi. The result was a masterpiece of synergy. The Sherman brothers' music inspired DaGradi as he created the storyboards, and DaGradi's storyboards inspired the creativity of the songwriting brothers. For example, when DaGradi showed Richard and Robert his drawing of a chimney sweep dancing while carrying his brooms, Robert said, "This is a song!" The result was the Oscar-winning "Chim-Chim-Cher-ee."

   Richard Sherman told me, "Walt believed in teamwork. We all chipped in and felt we were part of something special. We were proud to be on Walt's team, and this made us want to make *Mary Poppins* work. We all had our own little bailiwicks, but we felt free to make suggestions to each other and learn from each other."

Imagineer Rolly Crump tells a story from his days with Walt. Rolly was one of the key designers of the attractions Walt built for the 1964 New York World's Fair (notably, the "it's a small world" attraction, later installed at Disneyland). Walt loved Rolly's uninhibited creativity. After Rolly returned from the World's Fair, Walt stopped him in the hallway and asked where he had trained as an artist.

"Well," Rolly said, "I took art in high school…"

"No, no. Your formal training. Where did you go to art school?"

"When I was sixteen, I attended classes at a local studio for six consecutive Saturdays."

"That's it?"

"That's it."

"So where did you learn to do all that you've been doing?"

"I learned it from you."

"From me?"

"You have an open door policy at the studio. Anyone can go into any department and learn how the other animators and artists do their work. I did that while working in Animation."

Walt was pleased. "Roland," he said, "keep up the good work!"[98]

Because Walt broke down walls between departments, his studio was a creative community where artists, writers, musicians, actors, dancers, and filmmakers could lift each other to amazing heights of achievement. To lead like Walt, build teams, encourage new approaches, and enable people to swap jobs and to inspire each other. Not only will they surprise you, but they'll surprise themselves.

2. **Walt knew his people well.** Walt was constantly walking around, engaging in casual conversations, and getting to know his people as individuals. What are their goals? Their passions? Their hobbies? What books do they read? By showing an interest in your people, you'll learn they have ideas, interests, and hidden talents that can contribute to the success of your organization.

Walt took note of his best team players and matched them with creative people who could complement, motivate, and inspire them. Disney layout artist Frank Armitage told me, "The way Walt could combine people was amazing. He mixed people the way we mix paint. He knew how to put the right group of people together to produce the best results. In the early days, Walt would have writers, artists, and story artists all together in blue-sky sessions.... They built on each other's ideas and produced amazing results."

How did Walt assemble teams? He matched and paired contrasting skill-sets, contrasting personalities, contrasting styles, always hoping that something amazing would emerge from the meeting of opposites. He was rarely disappointed. He once said, "Of all the things I have done, the most vital is coordinating the talents of those who work for us and pointing them towards a certain goal."[99]

Remember how Walt described his role at the studio? "I go from one area of the studio to another, and I gather pollen and sort of stimulate everybody." He didn't wander aimlessly. He was purposeful in all of his interactions. He studied his people and came to understand them—in some ways, better than they understood themselves. This is a learnable leadership skill and a great way to discover hidden talent in your organization.

3. **Walt looked for passion and enthusiasm.** Walt not only recognized passion in other people, he inspired it. Walt's own passion was contagious. Like Walt, you can inspire that kind of passion and enthusiasm through your own example, by talking about your own commitment to lifelong learning and growth, by offering educational and training opportunities to your people, and by building a personal improvement mindset into the culture of your team or organization.

Who in your organization is genuinely excited to be there, passionate about achieving great goals, and committed to excellence? Who puts out extra effort and seizes every opportunity for personal and career growth? Passion is a sure sign of a person who possesses something extra.

In 1934, as the Disney studio was preparing to launch the *Snow White* project, Walt identified his core group of animators—his most talented, passionate, committed artists—and he put them through an intensive art training program, bringing in instructors from the Chouinard Art Institute. The art classes cost Walt $100,000 per year, and producers at rival studios sneered at Walt for wasting his money. They stopped sneering when *Snow White* was released in 1937.

Walt had created an organizational culture that was passionate about excellence and improvement. He looked for enthusiastic people, and he inspired them with his own creative passion. In the process, he elevated his studio to a far higher plane than the rest of the animation industry.

4. **Walt looked for clusters of skills and interests.** Walt never saw anyone as "just an animator" or "just a songwriter"—or even "just a nurse." Walt hired Hazel Gilman George to be the

on-call nurse at his Burbank studio—but as he got to know her, he learned that she was a multitalented woman with an array of valuable skills. She had excellent organizational skills, so Walt asked her to head up the informal investors group, the Disneyland Backers and Boosters.

Hazel George also had musical training and an interest in songwriting, especially as a lyricist. So Walt teamed Hazel with composers Paul J. Smith, George Bruns, and Jimmy Dodd, and she cowrote more than ninety songs for Disney TV shows and films. Under the name Gil George, she wrote songs for *The Mickey Mouse Club*, including "Talent Roundup," "Mickey Mouse Club Newsreel," and all the songs for the "Corky and White Shadow" serial. She also wrote songs for the films *The Light in the Forest, Perri,* and *Old Yeller.* Throughout her songwriting years, she continued to work full-time as the studio nurse.

Another example of Walt's ability to utilize every individual's cluster of talents is the Firehouse Five Plus Two, a Dixieland band drawn largely from the Disney studio creative staff. The band was formed by animator Ward Kimball in 1949 and performed and recorded until 1972. Though the band members maintained their day jobs with the Disney studio, they had an active schedule of live performances and recording sessions. They appeared on Walt's first TV special in 1950, *One Hour in Wonderland,* and made several appearances on *The Mickey Mouse Club.*

The "Firehouse Five" part of the band consisted of Ward Kimball (bandleader, trombonist, and sound effects man), animator Frank Thomas (piano), motion picture art director

Harper Goff (banjo), story man Ed Penner (tuba), and ani-mator Clarke Mallery (clarinet). The "Plus Two" part of the band consisted of professional musicians Danny Alguire (cor-net) and Monte Mountjoy (drums). Sound editor and Mickey Mouse voice actor Jimmy MacDonald sometimes played drums with the band, and Disney composer George Bruns sometimes subbed for Kimball on trombone.

The Firehouse Five Plus Two performed live at Disneyland on the televised opening day, July 17, 1955. The band could be seen performing in front of the Fire House on Main Street and also on the Rivers of America waterfront. Ward Kimball recalled, "Walt told us to wander around the park and play wherever there was a crowd. We were the first mobile band at Disneyland."[100]

Yet another example: Pinto Colvig was a clarinet and ocarina player in the music department at the Hyperion studio. He also had a rich baritone singing voice. One day, Walt walked into the music studio and heard the orchestra clarinetist doing his impression of a yelping dog—and Walt knew he'd found what he'd been searching for, the voice of Mickey's pal, Pluto.[101] Colvig went on to become the voice of Goofy, as well as Grumpy in *Snow White and the Seven Dwarfs*.

Today, there's a tendency to wall people off from each other in cubicles and departments. Workers have clearly defined job descriptions and all are expected to "stay in their lane." These organizations lose the benefit of all the talents and skills their people possess. Strict rules and tight control inhibit crea-tivity. An atmosphere of freedom, interaction, and teamwork unleashes creativity and reveals hidden talent.

Walt created an environment in which anyone could become a writer, tunesmith, musician, or Imagineer. Everyone drew ideas and inspiration from everyone else. There were no pigeon-holes at the Disney studio—just uninhibited creativity and synergy. The ability to spot talent and utilize it to the utmost was probably Walt's greatest people skill. You might even call it his leadership superpower.

Lead with Kindness

Walt was a paradox. I've interviewed hundreds of people who knew him. A few described him as a harsh and insensitive taskmaster. Most described him as the kindest man they've ever known. Some found him charming one day, then dour and distant the next. Most lived in awe of him. How could one man be remembered so differently by the different people who knew him?

In the early years of the Disney studio, Walt was sometimes sarcastic and demeaning toward his animators in front of their peers—a practice I abhor in any leader. One Disney historian suggested that Walt publicly humiliated his employees as a deliberate tactic to make it "easier to bend them to his will." I don't think so. Walt knew he had a quick temper and a sharp tongue—and he regretted it. "I've been a slave driver," he said in his later years. "Sometimes I feel like a dirty heel the way I pound, pound, pound."[102]

Walt's outbursts were usually triggered by pressure at the studio. In the early years, before the success of *Snow White*, and later, during the era of the strike and WWII, the studio often teetered on the brink of financial collapse. There were times when Walt and Roy would set up a card table and divide the studio's cash-on-hand among his workers.

Walt was deeply humiliated every time he had to stand in front of his employees with his pockets turned inside-out. Those pressures and emotions sometimes made him volatile, especially when his staff fell short of his expectations.

I think Walt disliked that trait in himself and he wanted to change it—and eventually he did. Most of the stories about Walt's short fuse came from those who knew him in the early years at the Hyperion and Burbank studios. Walt's temper was, I believe, a reflection of his quick-tempered father. When Walt demeaned one of his employees in public, he was exercising the same kind of harsh discipline his father inflicted on him. As a young entrepreneur, taking big risks and beset by multimillion-dollar worries, Walt responded in the only way he knew.

Bill Peet was a Disney story artist from 1937 to 1964. In his autobiography, Peet recalled that Walt "was never the same two days in a row." One day, Walt entered Peet's office and slumped in a chair with a deep sigh.

"What's on your mind, Walt?" Peet asked.

"It gets lonely around here. I just want to talk to somebody."

Walt told Peet about his boyhood, including his years delivering newspapers without pay for his demanding father. Walt reminded Peet of "a hurt little boy."

Peet was about to share his own boyhood "and let him know we had something in common"—but Walt abruptly sprang from his chair, muttering, "Gotta get going."[103] Perhaps Walt, who was notoriously guarded about his private life, suddenly felt he'd revealed too much.

By the mid-1950s, as the studio's financial problems receded, his outbursts of ill-temper became increasingly rare—though they didn't entirely disappear. Bob Gurr told me, "If Walt got upset with you, you'd get that forefinger of his rammed into your solar plexus. He'd get angry—but a minute later, he'd calm down."

Even though many of Walt's early employees found him difficult to work for, many Disney people I've interviewed admire and respect him for his toughness and his high standards of quality. Bob Kredel was a longtime Disney employee and a friend of Ward Kimball (Bob and Ward shared a fascination for antique steam trains). Bob told me, "The criticism most frequently aimed at Walt Disney was that he was a tyrant. Well, he was! Ward Kimball once said, 'Walt made us work. He drove us and pushed us and forced us to reach levels of perfection.' And you know what? Ward *admired* Walt for that!"

Walt's grandson, Walter Disney Miller, offered a balanced perspective on Walt's mercurial personality. "My grandpa wasn't always easy to work for," Miller told me. "He had a temper, and high praise wasn't his style. Yet people were drawn to him and wanted to please him. Many people on his staff stayed with him for twenty, thirty, forty years or more. He inspired loyalty."

It's true. As difficult as Walt could be, he inspired loyalty—partly by coming to the defense of his people. As one Disney animator told columnist Hedda Hopper, "Walt can be tough. But don't let anybody meddle with his artists. Most of them were trained here. They're his boys and girls."[104]

Rolly Crump joined the Disney animation staff in 1952 as an in-betweener, and eventually became a full-fledged animator on *Lady and the Tramp*, *Sleeping Beauty*, and *One Hundred and One Dalmatians*. In 1959, Walt sent Rolly to WED Enterprises to help design such attractions as Walt Disney's Enchanted Tiki Room and the Haunted Mansion.

"[Walt] had a childlike side," Rolly recalled, "a broad streak of kindness, that made you feel welcome in his presence, and that accounted in large part for his success." Rolly added that Walt "recognized the essential skills and talents of the people he assigned to work on his projects. He always picked the right people.... Once he chose you for a project, and once he knew you understood that project, he backed you to the hilt, no matter what others said. Walt seemed to always take my side despite his executives sometimes not sharing my opinions."[105]

Rolly recalled an incident during the design phase of "it's a small world." He had designed a clock for the façade of the attraction. The clock had a whimsical toy-like face with wheels for eyes, steepled brows, an angular nose, and a semi-circular smile. Rolly showed it to attraction planning executive Dick Irvine—and Irvine hated it. He told Rolly he was going to have Marc Davis redesign it.

So Rolly called Walt in and showed him the design. "That's good," Walt said.

"It doesn't have that European flavor," Irvine said. "I'm having Marc redesign it."

Walt looked sharply at Irvine and said, "I like it the way it is." Rolly always knew that Walt had his back.[106]

Most of the stories of Walt's kindness and compassion come from his later years, after he opened Disneyland. His regrets mellowed him, and he became much more charming, affirming, and supportive. He no longer humiliated his employees as he sometimes did in the 1930s and 1940s. To lead like Walt, learn from his early regrets and emulate those excellent people skills he displayed in his maturity as a leader.

Walt once said, "You can design and create and build the most wonderful place in the world. But it takes people to make the dream a reality."[107] Everything Walt achieved, he achieved through people. That's what leadership is: achieving amazing results through people. A leader must have people skills: the ability to delegate, the ability to motivate effort and inspire loyalty, the ability to create an atmosphere of creative freedom and informality, the ability to recognize and develop talent, and the ability to turn a collection of talented individuals into a unified team.

Delegating requires the ability to trust your people as Walt trusted his staff. He was the visionary, the motivator, the team builder—but it was his people who painted the background art, produced the beautiful animation drawings, wrote the unforgettable songs, and built the theme park. He recruited talented people and trusted them to produce the best work—yet he also kept tabs on the results. Leaders are responsible for both the successes and failures of the people they lead.

The proof of Walt's people skills and leadership genius is the fact that, no matter how many artists came or went, the quality of Disney entertainment products remained consistently high. Some have said that Walt was not an artist because after 1923 he didn't draw and animate anymore. Those who say that fail to understand Walt's unique kind of creativity. Walt's artistic medium was *people*. He expressed his creative vision through *people*. So Walt used his people skills to turn his vision into reality.

What can we learn about people skills from Walt's example? Here are the lessons I've identified:

1. **Get to know your people as unique individuals.** Engage them in casual conversation. Take a genuine interest in their families, their goals, their hopes and dreams. Ask people about their hobbies, interests, and hidden talents. Find out who they are and what they care about most. By getting to know people as unique individuals, Walt was able to uncover and utilize talents and abilities that his people didn't even know they had.

People don't all respond to the same incentives and motiva-tors. Some are motivated by money. Others crave recognition. Still others just want a simple pat on the back. Rolly Crump said that Walt brought out the best in everyone around him, and he did so by treating each person as a unique individual. Walt's daughter Diane recalled, "Dad wanted to take care of every-body. He wanted to know if an employee was sick or needed something. He knew about everybody's personal lives."[108]

2. **Win people over with charm and kindness—even when they intrude or interrupt.** Walt always treated autograph seekers as honored guests, not as intruders. He understood that "Walt Disney" was not merely a person—he was a walking corporate logo, and he made sure he represented Disney values at all times, even when it was inconvenient.

3. **Win people over by putting them at ease.** Walt knew that many people were nervous and star-struck in his presence, so he found ways of putting them at ease. You don't have to pull your tie askew or mash a pork pie hat on your head as Walt did. Instead, find a natural way to come across to others as a normal, friendly, approachable person.

4. **Build teams by pairing complementary individuals.** Great team chemistry takes place when you put people together in yin-and-yang combinations: match an introvert with an extrovert, a cerebral thinker with an uninhibited free spirit, a mechanical inventor with an abstract painter. Pair people with complementary personalities, skills, styles, and backgrounds—then watch the sparks of creativity fly. But make sure that every-one on the team is pumped up with passion and enthusiasm for your leadership vision.

5. **Lead with kindness.** Even when you feel pressured and stressed, make sure you don't take it out on your people. Treat the people you lead with kindness at all times. Be firm, set high standards, and hold people accountable—but do everything with compassion. Never humiliate or criticize your people in front of their peers. If anyone attacks or criticizes your people, become their defender. Let them know you've got their back, and they will repay you with loyalty and extra effort.

In 1929, shortly before Walt's twenty-eighth birthday, reporter Florabel Muir interviewed Walt for the *New York Daily News*. By that time, Mickey Mouse was a sensation, and the Disney studio was enjoying international success. Muir observed that Disney's Hyperion Street studio was "a headless company." She wrote:

> "Who's the president or head of this concern?" I asked.
>
> "We haven't any president or any other officers," Walt explained. "In fact, we are not even incorporated. I guess you couldn't call us a company. We just get together, the bunch of us, and work things out. We voice our opinions and sometimes we have good old-fashioned scraps but in the end things get ironed out and we have something we're all proud of."[109]

While it's not strictly true that the Disney studio was "headless"—Walt was in charge and everybody knew it—it is true that the studio was not run like a corporate hierarchy, with a corporate ladder. Walt was not at the top of the organizational pyramid, dictating memos from the corner office. Instead, the studio functioned as a community of relationships. Walt was in the middle of this creative community, always utilizing his people skills, always talking to his people, always asking questions and making suggestions and sparking ideas. Neal Gabler described the lesson Walt had learned from losing most of his animation staff to Charles Mintz in 1928—and how Walt's newfound people skills improved morale at the Hyperion studio:

> Having learned from his experience with the mutineers who detested him, Walt drew closer to his animators, stopping by their desks to talk not just about their work but about their interests and making suggestions to them without seeming overbearing. "The men loved it," [animator Ub] Iwerks said, "and they all responded."[110]

In 2005, for Disneyland's fiftieth anniversary, a first-story window was unveiled honoring Walt and the many cast members who have worked at Disneyland through the years. Located on a door to the left of the Main Street Cinema, the inscription on the glass reads, "Open Since '55—Disneyland Casting Agency —'It takes People to Make the Dream a Reality'—Walter Elias Disney, Founder & Director Emeritus."

It's a fitting tribute to Walt's people skills. Walt waved the wand and his people made Disney magic happen.

5

Walt's Good Character

In 1929, Mickey Mouse cartoons were hugely popular, yet the Disney studio was barely making ends meet. Walt's New York–based distributor, Pat Powers, seemed to be pocketing most of the profits. The meager checks Powers sent to Walt and Roy barely covered their expenses, and he refused to open his books for an audit. The Disney brothers hired attorney Gunther Lessing to protect their rights. Lessing, who had brokered a movie contract between Mexican bandit Pancho Villa and the Mutual Film Corporation, was known as a tough negotiator.

On January 17, 1930, Walt and Lillian boarded a train to New York. Walt believed Pat Powers had hidden an estimated $150,000 in royalties (equivalent to $1.5 million today), and it was time for a showdown. Walt went to Powers' Manhattan office and demanded an accounting. Powers said he would only open the ledgers if Walt signed a five-year distribution deal. When Walt scorned the offer, Powers told Walt he had hired Ub Iwerks away from Disney to animate a new cartoon series.

Walt couldn't believe it. He and Ub had been friends for more than ten years, ever since they founded Iwerks-Disney Commercial Artists in Kansas City. Walt had brought Ub to Hollywood, and Ub had remained loyal to Disney when Charles Mintz lured many Disney animators away two years earlier. Walt and Roy had given Ub a one-fifth share of the studio. How could Ub do this?

But Walt had ignored the fractures in his friendship with Iwerks. Ub resented Walt pressuring him to use in-betweeners (apprentice animators) to increase his productivity. Ub insisted on drawing every frame himself. And there was the time Walt saw Ub working on his car in front of the studio on company time. Walt had snapped, "Hire a mechanic and get back to the drawing board!" Ub said nothing but continued working on his car the rest of the day.

Ub felt he deserved more credit than "A Walt Disney Comic by Ub Iwerks." On one occasion, Walt and Ub were at a party, and a child asked Walt to draw Mickey Mouse. Walt told Ub to draw Mickey then Walt would sign it. Ub refused, saying, "Draw your own Mickey."[111]

Despite these warning signs, Walt hadn't realized Ub was seriously unhappy and ready to jump ship.

In September 1929, Charles Giegerich secretly approached Ub Iwerks, offering him a studio of his own and complete creative freedom. Who was Giegerich? He was supposedly working as Walt's bargaining representative in various distribution matters. In a clear conflict of interest, Giegerich went behind Walt's back to hire away his top animator. Iwerks agreed to sign with Giegerich, unaware that Giegerich secretly represented Walt's nemesis, Pat Powers.

On January 21, 1930, while Walt was meeting with Pat Powers in New York, Ub Iwerks went to Roy Disney and told him he was leaving the Disney studio, effective immediately. Roy was shocked. Like Walt, he had no idea that Iwerks was unhappy. Roy agreed to buy out Ub's share of the company, to be paid in installments (if Ub had not left the studio, his 20 percent share would have been worth millions during his lifetime).

Later that day, Walt wired Roy with the news: Pat Powers had hired Ub Iwerks away. When Roy learned that Ub had gone over to the enemy, he was livid.

On January 24, three days after resigning, Ub Iwerks returned to Roy's office. He told Roy he had signed a contract with Charles Giegerich—and had just learned that Giegerich had sold the contract to Pat Powers. Ub said he now regretted his decision and would not have signed had he known that Powers was behind it. Roy was relieved to know that Ub hadn't knowingly defected to Powers. But when Walt returned to the Studio, he could hardly stop talking about the "disloyalty" of Ub Iwerks.

Backed by Pat Powers, Ub opened the Iwerks Studio in 1930. But Powers had miscalculated. He thought that the reason for Disney's success was Ub Iwerks. He didn't realize that the creative force behind Mickey and the Silly Symphonies was Walt himself. Iwerks introduced two characters, Flip the Frog and Willie Whopper, but neither character caught on. The Iwerks Studio folded in 1936, and Ub produced several Porky Pig shorts for Leon Schlesinger.

By 1940, Ub was teaching animation at a vocational school. Disney animation director Ben Sharpsteen learned of Iwerks' situation and offered him a job at Disney, subject to Walt's approval. But first, Sharpsteen had to broker a reconciliation between Walt and Ub. On August 9, 1940, Ub lunched with Walt at the studio. Walt not only forgave Ub for his defection to Pat Powers, but never even mentioned it.

Walt was generous, allowing Ub to be his own boss, to roam the studio and tinker and experiment as he saw fit. Ub had lost interest in animation and wanted to develop new moviemaking technologies. His creative ideas contributed enormously to Disney films. Though Walt and Ub were not as close as they had once been, Walt was happy to have Ub back in the Disney studio where he belonged.

The Leader Who Forgives

The ability to forgive is an essential leadership quality and a crucial trait of good character. Walt exemplified forgiveness again and again in his leadership career. One of the most important examples was a crisis caused by conflict between Walt and Roy during the late 1950s.

Walt had created two companies separate from Walt Disney Productions: WED Enterprises (which built Disneyland attractions) and Retlaw Enterprises (a holding company that licensed Walt's name). WED owned the Santa Fe and Disneyland Railroad and the Monorail, and Walt Disney Productions paid WED to operate the attractions. Walt Disney Productions also had to pay Retlaw to use the Walt Disney name.

Roy thought Walt's demands could lead to a stockholder revolt and damage the Disney brand. He asked Walt for a meeting at Walt's Smoke Tree Ranch retreat so they could iron out their differences. The meeting turned acrimonious instead. As the Disney wives, Lillian and Edna, retreated to one end of the house, Walt and Roy were locked in a shouting match at each other. The battle lasted three days and ended in a stalemate. For an entire year after that failed peace conference, the Disney brothers communicated only through intermediaries.

Finally, Roy sent a delegation of attorneys to bargain with Walt and his agent. The meeting was a disaster, with Walt threatening to make movies for a rival studio and the studio attorneys threatening legal action. Roy heard the ruckus from his office down the hall. He had always defended his younger brother against bullies, and this was no exception. He stormed into the conference room and confronted the company attorneys.

"You forget how important Walt Disney has been to your careers," he said. "None of us would be here in this studio if it hadn't been for Walt. Your jobs, your benefits, everything you have are the result of Walt's sacrifices. He deserves a lot better treatment than he's been shown here today."

With that, the tone of the talks completely changed. Walt gave a little, the studio attorneys gave a lot, and Walt got most of what he wanted. The studio bought WED Enterprises and the rights to the Walt Disney name for $60 million. Walt retained Retlaw.

A few days later, Walt entered Roy's office with a birthday present —a Native American peace pipe. Roy laughed, filled the pipe with tobacco, and they smoked it together. Later, Walt sent a hand-written note to Roy:

> It was wonderful to smoke the pipe of peace with you again—the clouds that rise are very beautiful.
>
> I think, between us over the years, we have accomplished something—there was a time when we couldn't borrow a thousand dollars and now I understand we owe twenty-four million!

But in all sincerity, Happy Birthday and many more—and—
I love you.

Walt[112]

That pipe hung on Roy's office wall for the rest of his life, a symbol of brotherly love and Walt's forgiveness.

Forgiveness is just one trait in an array of qualities that make up good character. All successful achievements are built on a foundation of good character. It took all the strength of character Walt could muster to overcome setbacks (like the loss of Oswald the Lucky Rabbit), adversity (being chronically underfunded), and naysayers (both *Snow White* and Disneyland were once labeled "Disney's Folly"). Walt exemplified many other traits of good leadership character, including humility, generosity, integrity, persistence, a strong work ethic, tolerance, and optimism. Let's take a closer look at the role of good character in leadership.

Walt's Humility

Hollywood columnist Willa Okker visited the Hyperion studio in 1934 and published her impressions of Walt and his studio. She found him to be a man of great humility—and incredible creative energy: "Disney at thirty-two is . . . self-effacing, unassuming, prone to mitigate his place in the world—but the artist is a shaft of flame. Disney's white-hot enthusiasm is incendiary—you are caught up in his studio fire that dominates the atmosphere as soon as you step inside the studio gates."[113]

More than thirty years later, after Walt's death, filmland columnist Bob Foster recalled Walt in similar terms: amazingly creative yet deeply humble. In the 1950s, Foster was among a group of reporters and columnists who visited the Burbank studio for a preview screening of *The Mickey Mouse Club*. He wrote:

> The door quietly opened and a slender gentleman with graying hair slipped into the first seat in the back row.
>
> There was a sudden hush as everybody, especially those employed at the studios, turned their heads in the direction of the newcomer. It was the master himself, Walt Disney, visiting the viewing room.
>
> He motioned with his hand to start projecting and we saw some of the magic which has made him and his studio world famous.
>
> Just before the screening was over, I glanced to the back again and the seat was empty. That was as close as we ever got to him that day. I later did meet him. He was a shy man and wasn't comfortable with members of the press. He appreciated the press and was more than willing to talk with a columnist in his office, alone.... But to meet thirty or forty newsmen all at once was just too much for him.[114]

One sign of Walt's humility was his willingness to serve others. In 1942, Walt's friends Spencer and Louise Tracy founded a day care for deaf children in a bungalow on the USC campus. The following year, the Tracys transformed the day care into a private, nonprofit education center for preschool children with hearing loss, the John Tracy Clinic. Walt joined the board of directors in 1943 and was also a generous donor to the clinic. The clinic is named for the Tracys' son John, who was deaf due to Usher syndrome, a genetic disease.

Every year, the clinic held a fundraising luncheon, and Walt would often serve food and clear dirty dishes—a leading studio mogul taking the role of a busboy, the role of a servant. He cared about the work the

John Tracy Clinic did for deaf children, and he was humble enough to roll up his sleeves and do his part.

John Tracy, who passed away in 2007, attended the California Institute of the Arts, cofounded by Walt. John later worked in the art props department at the Disney studio in Burbank.

Though Walt was humble, he had a strong ego. Does that sound contradictory? It's not. There's a difference between having a *strong* ego and having a *big* ego. The word *ego* is Latin for "I." Walt had a strong awareness of his own self, his own purpose, his strengths and abilities, his talents and limitations. He didn't have an *inflated* ego, but he knew what he wanted to accomplish in the world.

Once, over lunch at the Burbank studio, Ray Bradbury told Walt, "I hear you're planning to redesign Tomorrowland. You know, I just helped design the United States Pavilion at the New York World's Fair. I have a lot of ideas. Would you hire me to consult on Tomorrowland?"

Walt said, "Ray, it's no use. It'll never work."

"Why not?"

"Because you're a genius and I'm a genius. We'd kill each other before the end of the week."

Walt had learned there was only room for one genius in his magical kingdom. Two geniuses meant two competing visions. He had the strength of ego to believe in his own vision. He was not arrogant or narcissistic. He was simply confident.

A humble leader with a healthy ego can be decisive, determined, and tough without being arrogant. A leader with a healthy ego can say in all humility, "I am good at what I do" or even, "I'm a genius." Walt wasn't bragging. He was stating the obvious.

Walt was demanding, yet those who worked for him often remained at his side for decades. How did Walt inspire such loyalty? I believe it was because of his essential humility. Beneath his strong ego and his intense drive to succeed, Walt possessed a basic farm boy humility that people found irresistible. Those who knew him best knew he was no self-seeking egotist. He was a humble genius who genuinely loved humanity. Such a leader is easy to love.

Walt's Generosity

On December 28, 1930, this headline appeared in the *Los Angeles Times*: "Orphans Attend Theater Party." The text read:

> Two hundred children of the Los Angeles Orphans' Home were guests yesterday at a theater party given by Walt Disney in cooperation with Hollywood Theaters, Inc., at the Filmarte Theater.
>
> Three Mickey Mouse sound cartoons were presented on one program for the first time in this country. In addition, the children viewed *The Lone Rider*, a western feature production. Each youngster was presented with a Mickey Mouse playball created for the Walt Disney studios and with toys furnished by Hollywood Theaters.[115]

From his earliest days in the motion picture business through his later years as a theme park impresario, Walt used his creations to benefit others. Walt's set decorator Emile Kuri recalled that, during one of his visits to Disneyland with Walt, they were sitting on the porch of City Hall when Walt perked up, leaned forward, and pointed to a pair of Catholic nuns entering the park, leading a group of orphans. Walt counted the children, then said, "Look at them all! Twenty-two of them!"

Walt leaped up and dashed over to the nuns. He introduced himself and said, "Wait right here." Then he rushed into City Hall. Moments later, he returned with the money the nuns had paid for admission plus a stack of free tickets for attractions. "Enjoy yourselves," he said. "I've made reservations for you to have lunch at the Plaza Inn, and you'll have hot dogs and hamburgers and malted milks and apple pie. You're my guests."

As the nuns and the children happily went on their way down Main Street, Walt sat down beside Emile. "They shouldn't have to pay to come in here," he said.[116] That was Walt, through and through. He was always generous, always eager to bless the lives of others with the products of his ingenuity.

In 1961, Walt and Roy provided a generous endowment to establish the California Institute of the Arts (CalArts) in Valencia, California —the first American degree-granting institution of higher learning devoted to the visual and performing arts. The Disney brothers also guided the formation of CalArts through the merger of the Los Angeles Conservatory of Music (founded 1883) and the Chouinard Art Institute (founded 1921). Since 1934, Chouinard instructors had helped train Walt's animators for the challenge of such projects as *Snow White and the Seven Dwarfs*, *Pinocchio*, and *Bambi*. The Los Angeles Conservatory of Music had trained many musicians and songwriters who contributed to Disney films. The two institutions officially merged in 1963.

Walt's vision for CalArts was much like his original vision for his animation studio: a community of the arts where talented people from many disciplines—artists, sculptors, writers, musicians, composers, dancers, and actors—could meet, learn from each other, and interact in a synergistic way. He explained his vision in a 1966 interview:

> Some of our most important discoveries have come from scientists who were searching for something else. That is the direction I would like CalArts to take. Students should be able to study the whole spectrum of

the arts. Perhaps a musician would find out he is more talented in art and vice versa.[117]

Walt was as proud of CalArts as he was of any of his other achievements, including *Snow White* and Disneyland. Why? Because Walt had a big, generous heart for future generations. He once said that CalArts was "the principal thing I hope to leave when I move on to greener pastures. If I can help provide a place to develop the talent of the future, I think I will have accomplished something."[118]

Walt's Integrity

John Hench worked for The Walt Disney Company for more than sixty-five years. He began his Disney career in 1939 as a story artist and went on to work in almost every area of animation, including backgrounds, art direction, effects animation, and more. He was Disney's official Mickey Mouse portrait artist, painting portraits for Mickey's milestone birthdays. He also worked in live-action films, notably as the designer of the giant squid for *20,000 Leagues Under the Sea*. He also helped design many Disneyland attractions.

During the construction of Disneyland, Hench helped design the Frontierland stagecoaches. Walt specified that the stagecoaches be 100 percent authentic, made of the same materials as stagecoaches of the Old West. Hench knew the Disneyland project was over budget, and the July 17, 1955 opening deadline was approaching. Hench suggested saving time and money by leaving off the leather-strap suspension of the stagecoach cab. "People aren't going to get this," Hench added.

"Yes, they will," Walt said sharply. "They will feel good about it. And they will understand that it's all done for them.... They will respond because people are okay."[119]

Hench got the point. Walt wasn't just building an amusement park. He was telling a story about the early American West, and he was going to tell it honestly. To do anything less would compromise his integrity.

Disney writer Charles Shows worked on the True-Life Adventures documentary series. While working on a film about African lions, he envisioned the perfect opening shot—a close-up of the open mouth of a roaring lion. Problem: the Disney location camera crews hadn't taken any such footage in Africa.

Shows went to Walt and said he could get the shot he wanted by taking a camera crew to the Griffith Park Zoo and getting "a close-up shot of the old boy's tonsils."

Walt responded, "You do, and you won't be here tomorrow."

Shows thought Walt was kidding—but the look on Walt's face was dead-serious. Walt explained, "We tell moviegoers that these nature films are shot in Africa. Not one foot of phony film is going into my nature pictures."

Charles Shows concluded, "It was honesty like this that makes Disney films worldwide favorites."[120]

A strong sense of moral integrity was central to Walt's motion pictures, as film historian John G. West observed:

> Walt Disney was neither a philosopher nor a classical dramatist, but he keenly understood that good ethics are an invariable part of good drama. "Good and evil" are "the antagonists of all great drama," he once observed. They "must be believably personalized." And in the ensuing conflict, "the moral ideas common to all humanity must be upheld."
>
> In his stories, they were.[121]

Walt was morally out of sync with Hollywood culture—and he knew it. Disney cartoons and feature films won many Academy

Awards in many categories, but only one—*Mary Poppins*—was ever nominated for Best Picture (it lost to *My Fair Lady*). Walt reflected, "Knowing Hollywood, I never had any hope that the picture [*Mary Poppins*] would get it. As a matter of fact, Disney has never actually been part of Hollywood, you know. I think they refer to us as being in the cornfield in Burbank."[122] Walt took justifiable pride in not being part of Hollywood. His studio reflected the moral integrity of Walt Disney himself.

Walt's Persistence

While the public thought of Walt as a millionaire filmmaker, the truth is that the Disney studio faced financial ruin again and again from its founding until the opening of Disneyland. After Walt's death, newsman Bob Thomas filed a retrospective on Walt's career, focusing on Walt's persistence. He wrote:

> At the time of his death last Thursday, Walt Disney's entertainment empire was so widespread and prosperous that it seemed impossible he had known times when his studio faced extinction.
>
> Yet until the last decade of his life, Disney was scorned by many financial minds who considered him a poor risk, a visionary who would bring his company to the edge of insolvency to accomplish dreams.
>
> For the first thirty years of his film enterprises, the pattern was the same: Walt got the ideas and his brother Roy got the money. But more than once the ideas outdistanced the money.[123]

Repeatedly cheated by distributors during the Mickey Mouse heyday, Walt and the studio operated on the edge of bankruptcy even while Mickey was taking the world by storm. It took every ounce of

Walt's perseverance and Roy's financial wizardry to get *Snow White* completed at a cost of $1.7 million. After the astonishing success of *Snow White*, the studio was briefly awash in cash. But Walt's newfound millions didn't sit in the bank very long. He built a plush new studio in Burbank and launched a spate of expensive new feature-length projects, as Thomas recounts:

> The euphoria that followed the success of *Snow White* sent Walt on a spending spree: *Bambi* cost $1.7 million, *Fantasia* $2.2 million, *Pinocchio* $2.6 million. Then Roy called a halt.
>
> "There isn't any more money, Walt," he told his brother. "Those new features wiped out all the profits that *Snow White* made, and our foreign market is knocked out by the war. We've got to tighten our belts."
>
> The Disney studio limped through the war, making training films and propaganda movies. Walt had a rough time gearing the studio for the peacetime market. He experimented with films that were a musical vaudeville and with movies that combined animation with live-action. None seemed to click.[124]

The Disney studio's struggle for survival was almost continuous from its founding in 1923 until the mid-1950s, when Walt bet everything—his studio, his home, his life insurance policy—on his Disneyland dreams. Walt's theme park was probably the biggest high-stakes gamble in the history of American business. It paid off, but not because Walt was lucky or because he wished upon a star. It paid off because Walt refused to quit. As Bob Thomas concluded, after Disneyland succeeded, "Roy Disney had little trouble finding the money to fulfill Walt's dreams."[125]

Everything Walt accomplished is a monument to his sheer dogged persistence in the face of adversity and opposition. Roy E. Disney,

Walt's nephew and Roy O. Disney's son, told me, "If Walt had one great gift, it was that he kept his head down and kept trying. Over the years he was told that his ideas were impractical, impossible, and would never work: 'Walt, you'll lose your shirt on *Snow White*,' or, 'Walt, give up this crazy obsession with an amusement park!' Walt knew his ideas were good and the naysayers were wrong. Walt proved that the only way to get things done is by sticking to your ideas and your beliefs."

As Walt himself once said, "I function better when things are going badly than when they're as smooth as whipped cream."[126] That's the persistent character of a great leader.

Walt's Work Ethic

Once in the 1950s, Walt left the Burbank studio, headed for his Smoke Tree Ranch hideaway near Palm Springs. A few hours later, one of Walt's studio employees looked up and saw Walt standing in the doorway. "Walt, what are you doing here?" the employee asked. "You're supposed to be resting in Palm Springs."

The boss grinned and said, "You know, the grass is awfully green around here."[127]

Walt was seldom happier than when he was in his element, going from one department of his bustling studio to another, inspecting, inspiring, motivating, and working. Or as another Disney associate told Hedda Hopper, "This studio is the palace which houses his fantasies. He can't stay away from it."[128]

For a 1957 profile of Walt Disney, columnist Charles Denton of the International News Service followed Walt around the studio for a day—and found the experience exhausting. Denton wrote:

Walt Disney might be called a relaxed dynamo. He works fourteen or more hours a day, seems to be everywhere at once at his factory of filmed fantasy, and rarely takes a vacation. During an ordinary working day, he moves quickly, from conference to sound stage, effortlessly readjusting his mind to handle each of an apparently endless series of problems as it arises. He sails along without an entourage of secretaries and side-men, without giving the impression that he is running, and without forgetting to stop for brief chats with his employees.[129]

In 1966, in one the last interviews before his death, Walt talked about the importance of hard work in achieving our leadership goals:

I formed my work patterns early in life. At first I worked on my father's farm, then I delivered newspapers in Kansas City for my father, who was a dealer. At fifteen I was a news butcher on trains that ran to Colorado and all over. At sixteen I was a night watchman in a jelly factory in Chicago.

Kids are too idle these days. Their parents don't think it's good for them to work when they're young, but that's a mistake. They have too much leisure, and they don't know what to do with it.

I worked hard as a youngster, but knew how to enjoy myself, too. When I did get some leisure, I used it to the utmost.

If you keep busy, your work might lead you into paths you might not expect. I've always operated like the princes of Serendip, who went on quests not knowing what they would find.[130]

To lead as Walt led, it's not enough to merely dream. You must build—and building dreams is hard work. But if you work hard enough and lead as Walt led, you can turn fairy tale dreams into real kingdoms.

Tom Connellan, author of *Inside the Magic Kingdom*, told me, "Some people are dreamers; others are builders. Walt was both—a unique combination. He didn't just dream. He executed his dreams. That's why the lessons of his life are so important to us today. We need people today who have the vision to dream as he did, plus the skills and the energy to pull it off and make the dreams come true."

Singer and actor Thurl Ravenscroft, whose voice can be heard in many Disney movies and theme park attractions, told me, "Walt was the greatest dreamer ever, but what made him so creative was that he saw his dreams through to fruition. Anyone can imagine a talking mouse or a castle in a park, but it takes hard work to make those dreams real. Walt made his dreams come true, and he was never satisfied until they were built the right way, exactly as he envisioned."

Thurl voiced many of the scalawags in Disneyland's Pirates of the Caribbean. He recalled, "One day, Walt walked me through the site and showed me where everything would be—the waterfall, the pirate ship, the burning town. He had dreamed it in exacting detail, and he was excited to watch it take shape.

"There's so much we can learn from Walt's life, but one of the most important lessons he teaches us is to dream big—then go after your dreams, see them through, build them, make them real. Walt is remembered to this day, not because he dreamed, but because he constructed what he had dreamed. When you walk into Disneyland, you enter his world of dreams. Walt's imaginary world is there for us to enjoy because, through hard work, he made it real."

What are your leadership dreams and goals? How hard are you willing to work to make them real? Walt inspires us to emulate his phenomenal work ethic.

Walt's Tolerance

When Walt signed Richard Fleischer to direct *20,000 Leagues Under the Sea*, he asked if Fleischer could recommend a screenwriter for the project. Fleischer replied without hesitation, "Earl Felton." Fleischer and Felton had worked together as director and writer on previous film projects, including *Armored Car Robbery* (1950), *The Narrow Margin* (1952), and *The Happy Time* (1952). Felton had lost the use of his legs due to childhood polio, but he got around very well with a crutch and cane.

Earl Felton had apparently made an enemy of someone at the Disney studio, because (as longtime Disney artist-Imagineer Herb Ryman recalled), someone tried to damage Felton's reputation by telling Walt that Felton was a Communist. This, of course, was at the height of the Red Scare and the McCarthy era. "Everyone knew that Walt was a committed anti-Communist," Ryman said. "Very patriotic and all that."

Felton's accuser, Ryman added, "thought that Walt would fire him or investigate him or kick him off the picture [for being a Communist]. Well, Walt's answer was, 'I'm glad to know that. It's a relief that he's a Communist. I thought he was an alcoholic.'"[131]

Walt hated Communism, and blamed Communist agitators for the strike that crippled his studio in 1941. Walt's tolerant attitude toward Earl Felton didn't mean he had gone soft on Communism. But Walt knew that many innocent people were being smeared by accusations of being a "Red"—and he had seen his own reputation dragged through the mud during the strike. He wasn't going to be swayed by a vicious rumor.

(As it turned out, Felton may have been an agent of the Central Intelligence Agency. In 1962, the Profumo scandal rocked Great Britain and ended the career of British government official John Profumo due to his relationship with nineteen-year-old model Christine Keeler.

Earl Felton was named in the scandal. In her 2001 autobiography, *The Truth at Last*, Keeler claimed Felton worked for the CIA.[132])

Tolerance and compassion for others was foundational to Walt's character. Yes, he could be short-tempered, but he always tried to be fair, even to those he disagreed with. He instilled those same qualities of tolerance and compassion in his two daughters. In a January 1943 letter, Walt told his sister Ruth:

> Little Diane is going to a Catholic school now, which she seems to enjoy very much. She is quite taken with the rituals and is studying catechism. She hasn't quite made up her mind yet whether she wants to be a Catholic or Protestant. I think she is intelligent enough to know what she wants to do, and I feel that whatever her decision may be is her privilege. I have explained to her that Catholics are people just like us and basically there is no difference. In giving her this broad view, I believe it will tend to create a spirit of tolerance within her.[133]

Walt's younger daughter Sharon said that her father was "a very religious man" but added, "He did not believe you had to go to church to be religious.... He respected every religion. There wasn't any that he ever criticized. He wouldn't even tell religious jokes."[134]

Walt had a genuine love for the human race, and he transmitted his values of love and tolerance through his movies, TV shows, and theme park.

Walt's Optimism

Ray Bradbury once wrote, "Walt Disney was more important than all the politicians we've ever had. They pretended optimism. He *was* optimism. He has done more to change the world for the good than almost any politician who ever lived."[135]

Walt's optimism enabled him to deal with painful childhood memories in a constructive way. Though he spoke candidly about the harshness of his boyhood in Kansas City, he never let his childhood pain darken his optimism. He shaped his memories around his idyllic years on the farm in Marceline, the thrill of his first circus parade, the joy of seeing the silent movie version of *Snow White* when he was a boy. He chose to emulate and honor his father's positive traits while choosing not to remember his father's quick temper, stern demeanor, and lack of understanding.

The 1960 Disney film *Pollyanna* is a distillation of Walt's optimistic outlook. People often use "Pollyanna" as a derisive term for someone who is naïvely, childishly optimistic ("Oh, don't be such a Pollyanna!"). But if you've seen the movie, you know that the title character, played by Hayley Mills in her first Disney role, is anything but naïve and child-ish. Walt's Pollyanna is a mature and well-grounded young lady who has endured incredible adversity, including the death of her parents. Yet her faith in God's love and goodness remains undimmed. Her life-affirming optimism transforms everyone she touches, including her unhappy Aunt Polly (Jane Wyman).

Pollyanna is a symbolic representation of Walt's own journey from a painful childhood to infectious optimism. Walt has spread his own optimism to the world through cartoons, feature films, television shows, and Disneyland.

If there was one glaring defect in Walt's makeup, it was his addic-tion to cigarettes. I'm not sure it's fair to call his smoking a "charac-ter flaw," but it was a habit that controlled him, a behavior he was unable to control. He acquired the smoking habit when he was a seventeen-year-old Red Cross ambulance driver in France. He usually smoked unfiltered Chesterfields or Camels. I'm told that a tobacco addiction is, for some people, every bit as hard to kick as a heroin addiction. For Walt, smoking became a three-pack-a-day curse that directly caused his premature death.

Over the years, family members and associates at the studio (including Hazel George, the studio nurse) urged him to quit. One Christmas, his daughter Diane gave him two cartons of filtered cigarettes, hoping the filters would help his chronic cough. Walt smoked them—but he broke off the filters before lighting them.

"I was Walt's friend," Art Linkletter told me, "but I failed him in one area. Many times I said, 'Walt, you've got to quit smoking.' He'd say, 'Art, I'm going to cut it out.' But he never did."

Disneyland employee Jim Haught told me about a time Walt walked into a warehouse at the Burbank studio. A worker in the warehouse didn't recognize him and said, "Sir, there's no smoking in this warehouse."

Walt raised an eyebrow. "Who says so?"

"Walt Disney himself."

Walt stubbed out his cigarette and said, "Well, that's good enough for me."

In his later years, Walt repeatedly tried to quit smoking, but without success. Hazel George occasionally brought doctors in to speak to the Disney staff about the dangers of smoking. She probably hoped the doctors might get through to Walt as well as the other smokers at the studio, but Walt never attended the lectures. He once told Hazel, "You're right about one thing: Smoking and drinking are sins. We're God's creatures and if we don't take care of the bodies he gave us, we're committing a sin."[136]

Walt was conscious of his position as a role model for the next generation. He never smoked in front of his guests at Disneyland,

and he adamantly refused to allow photos to be released that showed him smoking. Disney historian Jim Korkis once visited with Disney Archives with archivist Dave Smith, and he noticed several photos of Walt seeming to point with two fingers and a blurry white smudge curling in the air next to him. When Korkis asked what caused those smudges, Smith explained that they were puffs of cigarette smoke. The cigarettes had been airbrushed out of the photos, but not the smoke. Walt appeared to be pointing with two fingers when he was actually holding a cigarette. Some believe those doctored photos inspired the Disney company to train cast members to always point with two fingers, never with the index finger alone.[137]

Cigarettes robbed Walt of what promised to be his most creative and productive years—and they robbed the world of a utopian visionary.

Character under Fire

In January 2014, actress Emma Thompson received an award at the National Board of Review dinner for her work in the Disney motion picture *Saving Mr. Banks*. She portrayed *Mary Poppins* author P. L. Travers opposite Tom Hanks as Walt Disney. Unfortunately, actress Meryl Streep, who presented the award to Ms. Thompson, chose that moment to trash Walt's reputation.

Streep said that Walt, "who brought joy, arguably, to billions of people…had some racist proclivities. He formed and supported an anti-Semitic industry lobby."

That's simply untrue. The "lobby" Streep referred to was the Motion Picture Alliance for the Preservation of American Ideals (MPA). It was formed in February 1944 to defend the film industry from Fascist and

Communist infiltration. Other MPA members included John Wayne, Clark Gable, Gary Cooper, Ronald Reagan, Ginger Rogers, Barbara Stanwyck, Robert Montgomery, Victor Fleming, and John Ford. The roster of this supposedly "anti-Semitic" organization also included such Jewish notables as Ayn Rand, Morrie Ryskind, Bert Kalmar, Norman Taurog, and Cecil B. DeMille.

Walt joined the MPA for the same reason he made movies like *Johnny Tremain* and *Davy Crockett*, and for the same reason he built attractions like Great Moments with Mr. Lincoln: patriotism. The MPA was a patriotic, pro-America, pro-freedom organization, and no anti-Semitic actions have ever been taken by the MPA.

The MPA was falsely accused of anti-Semitism by a rival organization, the Council of Hollywood Guilds and Unions, formed in June 1944 *specifically* to counter the influence of the MPA.[138] Both the Council and the MPA promoted American values, but from different perspectives. The MPA was politically conservative, while the Council was politically liberal. Members of the left-leaning Council included Humphrey Bogart, Lauren Bacall, Danny Kaye, Walter Wanger, and Clifford Odets. They supported First Amendment free speech and feared that the MPA wanted to impose censorship on Hollywood. Unfortunately, the Council went too far, smearing Walt and other MPA members with charges of anti-Semitism.

I thoroughly debunked those anti-Semitism claims in *How to Be Like Walt* (2004). Neal Gabler also exploded those charges in his 2007 Disney biography. He concluded:

> Of the Jews who worked [at the Disney Studio], it was hard to find any who thought Walt was an anti-Semite. Joe Grant, who had been an artist, the head of the model department, and the storyman responsible

for *Dumbo*...declared emphatically that Walt was not an anti-Semite. "Some of the most influential people at the studio were Jewish," Grant recalled, thinking no doubt of himself, production manager Harry Tytle, and Kay Kamen, who once quipped that Disney's New York office had more Jews than the Book of Leviticus. Maurice Rapf concurred that Walt was not anti-Semitic; he was just a "very conservative guy." Still, when Tytle...joined the studio, he felt compelled to tell Walt that he was half-Jewish. To which Walt snapped that if he were *all* Jewish, he would be better.[139]

There's no evidence that Walt was a bigot, and there's an avalanche of testimony to the contrary. Yet these false accusations continue to circulate. Influential people like Meryl Streep have an obligation to check the facts before harming another person's reputation—especially someone who is no longer able to defend himself.

Meryl Streep also called Walt "a gender bigot." She cited "a letter from 1938 stating his company's policy to a young woman named Mary Ford of Arkansas, who had made application to Disney for the training program in cartooning." The letter read, in part:

Women do not do any of the creative work in connection with preparing the cartoons for the screen, as that task is performed entirely by young men. For this reason, girls are not considered for the training school. The only work open to women consists of tracing the characters on clear celluloid sheets with India ink, and then filling in the tracing on the reverse side with paint, according to the directions.[140]

The letter, signed by Disney employee Mary Cleave, is authentic. The text comes from the company's 1938 policy handbook. In that pre-feminism era, most companies discriminated against women. Employers reasoned that they would lose their investment in a woman employee when she quit work to start a family. I'm not defending that policy. I'm saying it was the cultural norm. Even Mary Cleave, the woman who signed the letter, apparently did not think the policy unfair.

Walt probably wasn't aware of the policy. He dealt with the creative side and left personnel and policy matters to Roy or Ben Sharpsteen. In fact, that policy goes against Walt's own stated position on women at the Disney studio. In a speech to his employees, February 10, 1941, Walt proudly stated that "we are training the girls" in the studio animation school, adding, "If a woman can do the work as well, she is worth as much as a man.... The girl artists have the right to expect the same chances for advancement as men, and I honestly believe that they may eventually contribute something to this business that men never would or could." He singled out three female artists for their outstanding contributions: Ethel Kulsar and Sylvia Holland for *Fantasia* and Retta Scott, a key animator on *Bambi*.

Clearly, Walt was decades *ahead* of his time in his treatment of women. He cited the principle of equal pay for equal work ("she is worth as much as a man"), equal opportunity ("the same chances for advancement"), and the idea that women artists would contribute a perspective "that men never would or could." There were many women animators, story artists, and background painters at the Disney studio in the 1930s and 1940s, including Mary Blair, art director for *Saludos Amigos*, *The Three Caballeros*, *Cinderella*, *Alice in Wonderland*, and *Peter Pan*. Other prominent women artists working for Disney during that era included Mildred Rossi, Thelma Witmer, Sterling Sturtevant, Bee Selck, Lorna Soderstrom, Fini Rudiger, and Gyo Fujikawa.

After Meryl Streep's remarks were reported in the press, longtime Disney animator Floyd Norman posted a thoughtful and balanced response on his blog. Norman, an African-American, listed many of the minority employees and women at the Disney studio during Walt's era, including Phyllis Hurrell, who ran the department that produced television commercials in the 1950s. He added:

> We already know women were not given the opportunities they deserved back in the thirties. This was not something practiced at Walt Disney Productions alone. This was true of American business in general. Despite that, the women of Disney's Ink & Paint Department have told me they've never had a better job. Were they denied the opportunity to compete with the boys over in the Animation Building? You bet they were. In spite of that, during the war years, young women proved they had what it took to compete with the big boys. . . .
>
> Walt Disney had his faults like the rest of us. . . . Like most of us, he continued to grow as he moved through life and in time he recognized women could compete alongside men. He knew that talent had no color or ethnicity and he judged people by their ability to do their job and do it well. Walt Disney was a man of his time, but he was determined not to be imprisoned by it. He dreamed of a better world and even had the audacity to try and build it. . . .
>
> In my fifty-plus-year career he was hands down the best boss I ever had.[141]

I hope that one day Meryl Streep will realize that the man she condemned as a "bigot" was truly one of the most enlightened leaders of the twentieth century. Making sure of one's facts is a crucial matter of honesty, integrity, and good character, as we have seen in Walt's own life. If Meryl Streep ever reads these words, I hope she'll investigate Walt's character with an open mind, reconsider her damaging words, and publicly retract them.

What can we learn about character from Walt's example? Here are the lessons I've observed:

1. **The ability to forgive is essential to effective leadership.** Few people ever wounded Walt more deeply than Charles Mintz, the film distributor who seized control of Walt's cartoon character Oswald the Lucky Rabbit. A few months after losing Oswald to Mintz, Walt went to Universal Studios to meet with an executive about a possible distribution deal for his new Mickey Mouse series. Entering the waiting room, Walt was surprised to find Charles Mintz sitting there, hat in hand, looking nervous and uneasy.

   Walt smiled broadly, put out his hand, and greeted Mintz warmly—as if the recent past was completely forgotten. They exchanged pleasantries, and neither Walt nor Mintz mentioned the Oswald matter. Later, Walt wrote to Roy and told him about his encounter with Mintz. "Poor old Charlie," Walt wrote. "It was sad to see him that way."[142] Walt not only forgave but actually pitied the man who had stolen Oswald from him.

   Writing in *Forbes*, entrepreneur David K. Williams (author of *The 7 Non-Negotiables of Winning*) called forgiveness "the least understood leadership trait in the workplace." At his software company, Fishbowl, "the innate ability to forgive" is woven into the culture. Forgiveness, he said, "cascades through everything we do and is recognized by those who work with us.... They know that when they make mistakes, we will help them overcome and learn new skills."[143] To be a leader of good character, be a leader who forgives.

2. **Be confident; believe in your abilities and your vision—but at the same time, be humble.** Animation preservationist Ron Stark told me, "Walt was just a plain, humble guy. He never took the attitude, 'I'm Walt Disney and I can do anything I want.' Walt's genuine humility made him accessible to everyone. He didn't put on airs. He was just a regular guy who played in his backyard with greasy trains. He worked in Hollywood, but he never 'went Hollywood.'" Walt had a strong ego, but not an inflated ego. His humility prevented his self-confidence from souring into arrogance.

3. **Be generous with your time and resources.** To Walt, money was worthless unless it could create happiness and benefits for other people. To lead like Walt, support people and causes you believe in. Use the products of your labor and ingenuity to bless other people. Every day, try to help someone who can never repay you or return the favor. Make generosity a daily habit.

4. **Guard your integrity.** Walt refused to compromise his integrity. No one would have known that Walt's documentary on African lions had one brief shot filmed at Griffith Park—but Walt would have known. He knew that integrity is an all-or-nothing proposition. He refused to compromise the truth, even in a seemingly inconsequential matter. Honesty and integrity are essential to good character, and good character is essential to great leadership.

5. **Never give up.** Persistence is essential to leadership. Surrender is not an option for a leader of strong character. Mickey Mouse, *Snow White and the Seven Dwarfs*, and Disneyland are all monuments to the rock-solid persistence of Walt Disney.

6. **Work harder than anyone else.** Walt was a dreamer—but none of his dreams would have come true without hard work. Dreams are as insubstantial as pixie dust. Hard work turns dreams into reality.

7. **Lead with tolerance.** Contrary to some of the revisionist smears spread about Walt, tolerance was one of his core virtues. Walt believed in religious tolerance, racial tolerance, and political tolerance. He celebrated diversity, and thought it was a benefit to humanity that we don't all look alike, think alike, and believe alike. He thought people of contrasting personalities, views, and backgrounds complemented each other and multiplied their contributions to society. If you lead your team or organization with a tolerant attitude, you'll reap the rewards of different ways of thinking, different ways of working, and different styles of creativity. A tolerance for differences is a key trait for success.

8. **Lead with optimism.** A positive outlook was essential to Walt's success. He imprinted his own optimism onto the personality of Mickey Mouse. At the same time, Walt never let his optimism outdistance his realism. He once said, "I always like to look on the optimistic side of life, but I am realistic enough to know that life is a complex matter. With the laugh come the tears, and in developing motion pictures or television shows, you must combine all the facts of life—drama, pathos, and humor."[144] An optimistic, can-do attitude is infectious. When you lead with optimism, you inspire confidence and enthusiasm in the people you lead.

Walt was a great leader because he was a good man who carefully guarded his good character. To lead like Walt, guard your good character. Opponents and misinformed critics may attack you and spread false rumors about you. But if like Walt you live well, maintain your integrity, and do good to others, your achievements and your good name will endure.

6

Walt's Competence

SNOW WHITE AND THE SEVEN DWARFS earned $8.5 million in its first release—the equivalent of more than $150 million dollars today. By 1944, with foreign markets closed by World War II, the Disney studio was struggling to survive. So Walt decided to re-release *Snow White* in an attempt to raise much-needed revenue. The studio spent hundreds of thousands of dollars on advertising, new Technicolor prints, and a publicity tour featuring Adriana Caselotti (the voice of Snow White), Clarence "Ducky" Nash (the voice of Donald Duck), and seven costumed dwarfs. Though *Snow White* was not as big a hit in re-release as it was the first time around, the Disney studio cleared a tidy (and much-needed) $1.41 million.[145]

Seven years later, Walt decided to release *Snow White* again. He preceded the 1952 re-release of *Snow White* with *The Walt Disney Christmas Show* on CBS on Christmas Day 1951.[146] The show broadcast clips from *Snow White* and featured an appearance by the Magic Mirror from *Snow White*, voiced by Hans Conried. Entertainment industry experts thought Walt had lost his mind. According to conventional wisdom, airing movie footage on TV damaged the film's value in theaters. No one would pay for a movie ticket to see a film they had already seen on television (even if it was just a short clip). But Walt viewed television as his marketing ally. Give people a taste of a movie on TV, and they'll pay for the whole meal at the box office.

Audiences proved Walt right. Television promotion made the 1952 re-release of *Snow White and the Seven Dwarfs* a huge success. Demand for the fifteen-year-old movie was so high that in one city in Australia, police had to be called to control the crowds that filled the streets in front of the theater. (Across the street, a theater showing a brand-new 3D movie was practically empty.)[147]

Walt used the profits from the 1952 re-release of *Snow White* to establish Disney's own distribution company, Buena Vista, and to launch a line of feature-length documentaries, the True-Life Adventures, beginning with *The Living Desert* in 1953.[148]

The Disney company released *Snow White* in theaters a total of nine times—in 1937, 1944, 1952, 1958, 1967, 1975, 1983, 1987, and 1993. According to Guinness World Records, those nine releases took in a total of $184,925,486 in the US alone—equivalent to $1.2 billion when adjusted for inflation.[149]

The popularity of *Snow White* both pleased and rankled Walt. He was happy that in 1937 he made one of the most popular and successful motion pictures of all time. But it bothered him that, for years, he was unable to top it. In 1953, one of his associates at the Disney studio told Hedda Hopper, "I think the perennial success of *Snow White* annoys him. He's determined to top that picture, but every time it's reissued, the film is more successful than ever."[150]

In fact, it wasn't until 1964 and the release of *Mary Poppins* that Walt was finally able to top *Snow White*.

A great leader must start with a *vision*, must have the *communication skills* to convey that vision to the team, must have the *people skills* to motivate and energize the team, and must have the *good character* to build a bond of trust with the team. But the first four sides of leadership can't help a leader who lacks the fifth side of leadership: *competence*. I define competence as the ability to compete, the desire to strive for excellence, the drive to pursue and achieve great goals.

Walt had an intense competitive drive, an obsessive need to keep topping his earlier achievements. Walt wasn't competing against other filmmakers. No other filmmaker was in his league. Instead, he was constantly competing against himself. He was relentlessly pursuing excellence in everything he did, whether it was a seven-minute cartoon, a feature-length motion picture, or the world's first theme park.

Walt's Ability to Summon a Performance

In addition to his long Disney career, Thurl Ravenscroft was the voice of the Kellogg's Frosted Flakes mascot, Tony the Tiger. As the bass singer of the Mellomen quartet, Thurl can be heard in *Alice in Wonderland*, *Lady and the Tramp*, *Cinderella*, and other Disney classics. He recalled Walt's intense commitment to excellence, noting that Walt was personally involved in every recording session.

"He knew what was right, what was wrong," Thurl said. "He knew what he wanted, what he didn't want. So he was in every session. And he took a liking to me. Every time he came up with an idea, he'd say, 'Let's see what Thurl will do with it.'"

From Disneyland's opening day, Thurl's voice has been heard all around the park. "Oh, I did so many things at Disneyland," he said. "The train that went around the park. 'Howdy, folks, and welcome aboard the Disneyland Railroad!'... And Bear Country Jamboree. I was the buffalo head on the wall.... Pirates of the Caribbean, I was many of the drunken pirates." The Mellomen quartet also sings in the graveyard sequence of the Haunted Mansion, with Thurl's face appearing as one of the singing statues.

Thurl and the Mellomen performed the music for an unforgettable scene in *Lady and the Tramp*—the dog pound scene in which a quartet of dogs sing a mournful rendition of "There's No Place Like Home." It's a touching scene that somehow manages to be hilarious and heartbreaking at the same time. The bars of the dog pound cast shadows across the dogs, making them appear to be wearing striped uniforms. The scene was Walt's idea, and Thurl described how Walt summoned the performance he wanted:

"Walt said, 'I'm going to make a picture with a prison scene. But it's going to be dogs. And the dogs have to howl in four-part barbershop harmony. Can you do it?' We said, 'All we can do is try, Walt.' So we messed around with it, and Walt was in the session.

"Finally, he said, 'It sounds wonderful, guys, but it still sounds like human beings howling like dogs.' We said, 'Walt, why don't you go up to your office and have lunch. We'll have lunch, then we'll work on it again. We'll call you back when we think we have something. So we stayed in the studio and he went up to the office and we messed with it and we recorded various things. Finally, we said, 'Hey, that sounded like real dogs!'

"So we called Walt down, and he sat in that big sound stage with three Voice of the Theater speakers around him, and we played it. And I looked at Walt and there were tears running down his cheeks, and he said, 'Don't touch a thing! You did it!' And that was typical of Walt. He knew what he wanted, and he wasn't happy until he got it. He knew it sounded like dogs howling."[151]

One of Walt Disney's most important leadership skills was his ability to summon the performance he needed from an artist, an actor, or a musician. How did Walt acquire this skill? Answer: through years and years of practice.

His first attempts to summon a performance took place in the early 1920s when he was making the *Alice Comedies*, combining live-action footage of a child actress with the antics of cartoon characters. Virginia Davis, the original Alice in the *Alice Comedies*, shared a fascinating insight with me: Walt summoned her performance by acting out the role himself.

"Walt was an excellent storyteller and actor," she said. "He would act out the character, so I could see the kind of performance he wanted. He'd say, 'Let's pretend there's a lion chasing you. Here it comes! You're frightened! Now scream!' Or he'd pretend to be a wolf and roar, 'Arrgghh!' Because they were silent films, he could direct me out loud while the camera was rolling."

When Disney was building attractions for the 1964 New York World's Fair, Walt again demonstrated his ability to summon a performance. The Illinois state exhibit for the Fair was "Great Moments with Mr. Lincoln," featuring an Audio-Animatronics version of President Abraham Lincoln. Walt took a big risk in accepting the assignment.

The technology of Audio-Animatronics was in its infancy and had only been used to animate talking birds in Disneyland's Enchanted Tiki Room. Yet Walt had promised his sponsors that Lincoln would speak and move convincingly.

To program the robot, Walt's Imagineers filmed actor Royal Dano delivering a speech by Lincoln, using the actor's gestures and expressions as a reference. In the first take, Dano gave an excellent reading—but Walt shouted, "No, no! That's not what I want!" The actor did additional takes, and each time Walt was displeased. Finally, tired and discouraged, Dano seemed unable to go on.

At that point, Walt stood and led the entire studio crew in singing "The Battle Hymn of the Republic." It was an electrifying moment. As crew members wiped away tears, Walt cued Royal Dano—and the ghost of Lincoln spoke through him. When people visited "Great Moments with Mr. Lincoln," they were astonished and moved by the emotional power of Mr. Lincoln's performance. After the New York World's Fair, Walt brought Mr. Lincoln to Disneyland's Main Street Opera House, where it opened on the park's tenth anniversary, July 17, 1965.

Walt's ability to inspire and motivate his actors, writers, composers, and artists to deliver the performance he wanted is a vivid example of Walt's competence to lead. How did he acquire this ability? He never went to business school. In fact, he never finished high school. He was completely self-taught. He learned everything he needed to be a leader the same way you and I can: through reading, talking to people, gaining hands-on experience, and following curiosity wherever it leads.

Walt's Commitment to Continuous Learning

Walt Disney's accomplishments as a business leader and entertainment mogul have never been equaled. One of the greatest innovators of the twentieth century, Walt produced the first cartoons that talked, the first cartoons in Technicolor, the first feature-length animated cartoon (*Snow White*), the first motion picture with multichannel sound (*Fantasia* in Fantasound), and the first wide-screen animated cartoons. Walt holds the all-time record for the most Academy Awards—fifty-nine nominations and twenty-six Oscars (twenty-two competitive awards and four honorary awards). He even created the first TV infomercial with his *Disneyland* documentary on the making of *20,000 Leagues Under the Sea*.

Walt invented a new kind of entertainment experience—the theme park—when he opened Disneyland in 1955. Soon after it opened, Disneyland become the top tourist destination in America. Walt invented and patented the technology known as Audio-Animatronics, which brought birds to life in the Enchanted Tiki Room, repopulated the Caribbean with pirates, and resurrected a beloved American president. He held patents for a number of inventions, and he revolutionized transportation with his Disneyland Monorail and PeopleMover systems.

Walt cofounded a private university, California Institute of the Arts (CalArts). He played a top leadership role in the 1960 Winter Olympics and the 1964 New York World's Fair. Before his death, he began developing another innovative park in Florida, Walt Disney World, featuring a new kind of city, the Experimental Prototype Community of Tomorrow, or EPCOT.

This is an amazing list of accomplishments for a self-taught farm boy from Missouri. How do you explain it? His friend Art Linkletter offered this simple explanation: "Walt had the mind of a child. He was so curious."[152] In an interview a few months before his death, Walt talked about his natural curiosity and his commitment to lifelong learning:

> I've always had a great deal of natural curiosity. Whenever I was curious about something, I'd go to the library and ask for all the books they had on that subject. I'd read about everything, and then I'd ask questions from people who were experts in their field.
>
> When I started cartoon films, I asked the older artists how they did things. Some of them didn't want to give me any secrets of the trade, but most of them gave me all the help I needed.
>
> I do the same thing today. If I'm curious about something, I pick up the phone and call someone who knows about it. I always get an answer. You'd be surprised how nice people can be when you show them you're really interested.[153]

Walt absorbed knowledge, ideas, and inspiration from everybody around him. During construction of Pirates of the Caribbean, which begins in a simulated Louisiana bayou, Walt learned that one of his construction workers was born and raised in the bayou. Walt walked the man through the attraction and asked: Is it realistic? Are the details right? It was good, the man said, but something was missing, yet he couldn't put his finger on it.

They walked through the attraction again—and this time the man said, "Fireflies! There ought to be fireflies in the swamp!" A few days later, the swamp was alive with electric fireflies.

Some of Walt's best ideas came to him during his travels around the country or overseas. When he traveled, he didn't sightsee—he researched new ideas and new projects. After a European vacation in 1957, he returned to the Burbank studio bursting with energy and ideas. He confessed to newsman Bob Thomas, "I'm a lousy tourist."[154]

Walt was fascinated by mechanical gadgets. In mid-1949, Walt, Lillian, and their daughters Diane and Sharon vacationed in Europe. During the Paris leg of their adventure, Walt went out on his own, leaving his wife and daughters at the hotel. He returned with two shopping bags bulging with mechanical toy animals. Walt and the girls wound them up and sent them rolling, crawling, and clanking across the floor. The girls were entertained—but Walt studied the toys. He told Lillian, "It's amazing that you can get such interesting movement from a very simple mechanism."[155]

A year or so later, Walt and Lillian visited one of their favorite cities, New Orleans. They wandered into an antique shop, and Walt was instantly captivated by a mechanical caged bird. It whistled and chirped, moved its head and wings, and opened its beak in sync with a trilling bird song. Walt bought the mechanical bird and took it home to California. He presented it to his studio machinist Roger Broggie and sculptor Wathel Rogers (who would later become Walt's first Imagineer) and asked them to disassemble it and find out how it worked.

They discovered that the bird was operated by a wind-up spring that turned a series of cams and gears. One cam caused the wings to flutter, another operated the beak, another moved the head, another produced the tweets and chirps. It was an ingenious mechanism. When Broggie and Rogers demonstrated how the bird's innards worked, and how compact it all was, Walt instantly saw the possibilities. If an anonymous toymaker from the past could build such a convincingly real bird out of cams, gears, and a wind-up spring, why shouldn't his studio engineers build a mechanical man?

In 1951, Walt hired actor-dancer Buddy Ebsen to perform a dance routine in front of a white screen marked in black gridlines spaced twelve inches apart. Walt acted out the movements he wanted Ebsen to make, and Ebsen followed Walt's lead, performing a dance routine while 35mm movie cameras recorded his movements from three angles at a rate of twenty-four frames per second. After the session, each frame was enlarged, studied, measured, and mathematically analyzed so that Broggie and Rogers could build a nine-inch-tall dancing mechanical man using the gear-and-cam technology of the mechanical bird.

This effort, known as Project Little Man, was a forerunner of Audio-Animatronics.[156] Walt put Project Little Man on hold when he assigned his Imagineers to begin building Disneyland.[157]

Walt's Enthusiasm for Ideas and Imagination

Walt's greatest area of leadership competence was his ability to coach and magnify the creativity of others. He was a spontaneous generator of ideas, and he was a sponge for the creative ideas of others. Longtime Disney film editor Stormy Palmer told me, "Walt would listen to all of us in the meetings, and he would let you know if he thought you were wrong. But he would think about what you said. Later, he might see you in the hall and say, 'Well, maybe you were right. Why don't we go back and take another look at your idea?' He had his own ideas, but he was always willing to listen to new ideas. Walt was a good listener."

Nothing stirred Walt's enthusiasm like a great idea whose time had come. "You go through stages with an idea," he told interviewer Charles Denton. "First, you're uncertain. Then you get excited, and then worried. When you start making commitments, you get panicky. Here you'll have people hired and ready to start a thing, and you won't know whether you'll be ready to start it on time. It's very exciting."[158]

Once Walt was committed to an idea, such as *Snow White* or Disneyland, he had to fight for it. He told Denton ("in a voice tinged with eagerness," the reporter observed), "You get an idea, and you just can't wait. Once you're started, then you're in there with the punches flying. There's plenty of trouble, but you take it. You can't back out. It gets you down once in a while, but it's exciting. I think the whole business is exciting." Denton added, "In this spirit of excitement, Disney has risked millions, altered the course of motion picture history, helped bring about three-network competition in TV, [and] gained international influence."[159]

A creative leader is constantly observing and never wastes an experience. The 1931 Mickey Mouse short *Traffic Troubles* was inspired by a traffic ticket Walt received from an L.A. cop. Walt was on the way to work when he was ticketed, and he came into the studio dratting and fuming. As his animators gathered around him and listened to his tale of woe, Walt realized that to them, at least, it was a hilarious story. Since Mickey was Walt's alter ego, it was only natural that Walt's traffic stop would become the kernel of a Mickey Mouse cartoon.

Walt assigned *Traffic Troubles* to David Hand, an experienced animator who had worked at the J. R. Bray and Walter Lantz studios before coming to Disney. Hand told interviewer Michael Barrier, "I had a particular Mickey Mouse taxicab scene to do [for *Traffic Troubles*], and I did my very best with it.... [I] got it on the Moviola with Walt, and he squinted and squirmed and grunted, and said, no, it didn't have enough exaggerated action to it. I said okay, and back I went to my desk."

Hand redrew the scene, making the action wilder and more exaggerated. He showed the pencil test to Walt—and Walt rejected it again. Still not exaggerated enough. Hand redrew the same scene *five times*, each version more exaggerated than the one before. Each time, Walt rejected it. More exaggeration!

David Hand recalled, "I thought, 'What does this crazy man want?' I'd been in the business eleven years then, and Walt had much less time in the business.... I just thought that he ought to know that this animation of mine is acceptable, that was all."

Finally, David Hand decided he'd show Walt how wrong he was. "I said, 'I'm going to make this thing so extreme, so outlandish, so crazy, that he'll say, 'Well, Dave, I didn't mean to exaggerate it *that* much.' So I did.... I made that thing so outlandish, and so extreme, I was ashamed of what I had done. But I brought the new test in very self-righteously and put it on for Walt, and said, 'All right, Walt, I did this thing over again, I hope it's okay,' while slyly watching for him to explode."

Walt put the film loop on the Moviola and watched it, again and again and again. Finally he looked up with a broad grin and said, "You've got it! Why didn't you do it that way in the first place?"

Hand recalled, "That lesson stuck with me."[160] As he progressed in his Disney career and became a supervising animator, David Hand taught that same lesson to the young animators he supervised: Uncork your imagination. Unleash your creativity. Let go of your inhibitions. Go wild and exaggerate. That was Walt's approach to creativity, and David Hand adopted it as his own.

Most of our creative limitations are self-imposed. We limit ourselves by worrying about what other people will think. The moment we place limits on our imagination, we inhibit our creativity. "I must explore and experiment," Walt said. "I am never satisfied with my work. I resent the limitations of my own imagination."[161] And so should we.

Creativity is not so much a natural talent as a learnable state of awareness. I interviewed Disney story artist Joe Grant, whose Disney career began with *Snow White and the Seven Dwarfs* (1937). He told me, "[Walt] had an astounding creative awareness. He not only stored up ideas and material in his mind, but he was alert to ideas and story material in the world around him. He was thinking and creating on many different levels, at all times, twenty-four hours a day. It was exciting and stimulating to be around him, because ideas were constantly whirling around him. If you stood next to him, you caught some of his creative awareness. You began to see the world the way he saw it. You began to inhabit his world of ideas."

A creative mind is an open mind. As Walt wrote in an article for *The Journal of the Society of Motion Picture Editors* (January 1941):

How very fortunate we are, as artists, to have a medium whose potential limits are still far off in the future; a medium of entertainment where, theoretically at least, the only limit is the imagination of the artist. As for the past, the only important conclusions that I can draw from it are that the public will pay for quality, and the unseen future will take care of itself if one just keeps growing up a little every day.

The span of twelve years between *Steamboat Willie*, the first Mickey with sound, and *Fantasia*, is the bridge between primitive and modern animated pictures. No genius built this bridge. It was built by hard work and enthusiasm, integrity of purpose, a devotion to our medium, confidence in its future, and, above all, by a steady day-by-day growth in which we all simply studied our trade and learned.[162]

Creative thinkers question assumptions and willingly set aside cherished beliefs and certainties to take an intuitive leap into the unknown. Uninhibited imagination, fueled by enthusiasm, disciplined by a strong work ethic, empowered by confidence and commitment, took the Disney studio from *Steamboat Willie* to *Fantasia*, then on to *Sleeping Beauty* and *Mary Poppins*. Had he lived to see the era of *Toy Story*, *Finding Nemo*, and *Cars*, he might have been amazed.

But then again, perhaps he saw it coming all along.

Walt's Disdain for Sycophants

Even though Walt would challenge new ideas, he still wanted to hear every point of view. He respected people who defended their ideas with facts and logic. Imagineer Rolly Crump tells a story that speaks volumes about Walt's respect for people with minds of their own—and his disdain for sycophants and yes-men.

Walt once had a breakfast meeting with some of his executives at a restaurant. The waitress came to take their orders, and the first executive ordered ham and eggs.

The waitress turned to Walt.

"I'll have waffles topped with strawberries," he said.

Immediately, the first executive piped up, "That sounds really good! You know what? Change my order to waffles with strawberries on top."

The next executive said, "That *does* sound good. I'll have waffles with strawberries on top."

The next executive in line: waffles with strawberries.

The next exec, ditto.

Walt stood up, tossed down his napkin, swore vividly, and walked out of the restaurant without breakfast. The meeting was over.[163]

After all, what was the point of the meeting? If those executives didn't have the strength of their own convictions when it came to ordering breakfast, how were they going to offer any useful ideas for running a studio or a theme park? Why have a meeting at all?

Walt conducted countless meetings over the years. He didn't believe in wasting time or going through the motions. One of the most basic chores of leadership is chairing meetings, and Walt's goal in every meeting was to maximize the creativity of every participant. A meeting led by Walt always began and ended on time. He welcomed new ideas and dissenting views—but he tolerated no dissent once he had decided a matter.

The give-and-take at Disney meetings could be rough on a subordinate's ego. Dick Nunis, former chairman of Walt Disney Parks and Resorts, recalled a confidence-shaking meeting early in his Disney career. "I was giving this pitch to Walt," Nunis said, "and he was just killing me. He said, 'Nunis, you don't know what you're talking about,' and walked out of the room. Everybody followed him, and I sat there in this big room all by myself. I thought I had been fired and was thinking of where I could go to get a new job when I heard the door open behind me. It was Walt. He put his hand on my shoulder and said, 'Look, young fella, you keep expressing your opinions; I like it.'"

Nunis believed that Walt tested his subordinates to see who were yes-men and who had the confidence to express their honest views. "I think the people who stuck to their guns," Nunis concluded, "whether they were right or wrong, were the people he respected the most."[164]

Walt's brother Roy agreed—Walt did not like yes-men. He wanted honest opinions from people who knew their own minds. Roy recalled, "Once, after viewing a new cartoon with evident displeasure, Walt called for comments from a group of our people. One after another they spoke up, all echoing Walt's criticism. 'I can get rubber stamps that say, "Yes, Walt,"' he snapped."[165]

Walt's Obsession with Quality

Less than a year and a half after the creation of Mickey Mouse, Disney cartoons were widely recognized as vastly superior to the output of other studios. In March 1930, *The London Observer* published its appraisal of Disney animation, "The Cartoon and the Age," comparing Walt's Mickey Mouse and Silly Symphonies to the works of Shakespeare, Goethe, and Beethoven:

There are some names in every art and every industry that seem permanently fixed on the tip of the tongue. If we talk long about literature we are sure to return, sooner or later, to the mention of Shakespeare and Goethe. If we talk about motor-cars, we shall inevitably come back to Ford. Music cannot leave Beethoven and Wagner alone, and a discussion of architecture will inevitably veer round to Eiffel and Le Corbusier. As for the cinema... if the conversation is in the least intelligent, it will touch again and again on Chaplin and Sennett, Pudovkin and Eisenstein, Lubitsch and Disney—the small group of artists who, living fully in their time, have known how to give their work a value beyond topicality, cutting clear through all the extravagance to the bare essentials of the screen. . . .

Disney has made the drawn film the fashionable pastime of intelligence. . . . Only Disney, of all the cartoonists whose work I know, has the real sense of rhythm and composition, the real feeling for beauty, the real instinct for comic criticism—his drawings are the only ones held in by their limits and pushed to the full scope of their possibilities, fully controlled and so complete.

[Australian operatic soprano] Miss Florence Austral is said to have complained the other night that the public is neglecting Mozart for Mickey the Mouse—as though that were the extreme measure of popular stupidity. For my own part, I can think of nothing in modern entertainment for which Mozart could be more fitly neglected. Disney's cartoons are right for the age.... Disney draws his cartoons under the influence of contemporary Western thought, and their popularity is really a testimonial to the mass instinct for what is good and true.[166]

At the same time Disney's cartoons were being praised as Mozart-level entertainment, Walt was urging his animators to aim even higher. In 1941, looking back on the era of the late 1920s and early 1930s, Walt recalled: "Some of the possibilities in the cartoon medium had begun to dawn on me. And at the same time we saw that the medium was dying. You could feel rigor mortis setting in. I could feel it in myself. Yet with more money and time, I felt we could make better pictures and shake ourselves out of the rut."

Walt reflected that when he let go of Oswald the Lucky Rabbit and invented Mickey Mouse, "[I] made my Declaration of Independence and traded security for self-respect. An artist who wouldn't is a dead mackerel. Thereafter, we were to make pictures for quality and not for price. The public has been willing to pay for this quality." The result of Walt's obsession with quality was that the Disney studio became more like a center of learning and artistic expression than a mere cartoon factory. Walt wrote:

In our little studio on Hyperion Street, every foot of rough animation was projected on the screen for analysis, and every foot was drawn and redrawn until we could say, "This is the best that we can do." We had become perfectionists, and as nothing is ever perfect in this business, we were continually dissatisfied.

In fact, our studio had become more like a school than a business. As a result, our characters were beginning to act and behave in general like real persons. Because of this we could begin to put real feeling and charm in our characterization. After all, you can't expect charm from animated sticks, and that's about what Mickey Mouse was in his first pictures. . . .

Each year we could handle a wider range of story material, attempt things we would not have dreamed of tackling the year before. I claim that this is not genius or even remarkable. It is the way men build a sound business of any kind—sweat, intelligence, and love of the job. Viewed in this light of steady, intelligent growth, there is nothing remarkable about *The Three Little Pigs* or even *Fantasia*—they become inevitable.[167]

Walt continually analyzed the films his studio produced. By 1949, Walt recognized that there was a manic energy and hilarity in those early Mickey Mouse cartoons that was lost as Mickey—and the animators who drew him—matured. "We haven't the pace we once had," Walt Disney told columnist John Crosby. Though the early Mickey Mouse cartoons were primitive by post-WWII animation standards, audiences found them more entertaining than the full-color, technically advanced Mickey Mouse cartoons of the late 1940s. Walt added, "The exhibitors tell us that the audience hasn't changed but we have."[168]

The result of this introspection was Walt's decision to let Mickey become less of a cartoon star and more of a Disney corporate logo. By the 1950s, Mickey was seen mostly in cameo roles. Even in an official Mickey Mouse cartoon such as *R'coon Dawg* (1951), it was Pluto, not Mickey, who took center stage. The last regular Mickey Mouse cartoon,

The Simple Things, was released in 1953. It would be thirty years until Mickey's next starring role, in *Mickey's Christmas Carol* (1983). Diane Disney Miller recalled:

> As Mickey became more of a celebrity, there was a distinct change in his character and his behavior.... When you look at the early Mickey, he did...all these almost vulgar things, but as he became more famous, as Dad said, there were a lot of things that he didn't think Mickey should do because he was the emblem of the company. And so that's when they invented Donald Duck and Goofy to do all those things.... Dad himself said he [Mickey] got us out of trouble when things were really low, and he was a symbol of laughter. But now he's simply sort of a host in his little tuxedo.[169]

Walt was eternally grateful to Mickey for saving the Disney studio from disaster in 1928. But when he realized that his beloved Mouse had lost his edge of wild hilarity, he allowed Mickey to retire from acting and become the studio's Mouse Emeritus. It was undoubtedly a difficult decision for Walt, but it was consistent with his obsession for quality.

Quality-Conscious, Not Cost-Conscious

Frank Thomas joined the Disney studio in September 1934 as Disney employee number 224. Later known as one of "Disney's Nine Old Men," he came to Walt's attention when he animated the 1937 Silly Symphonies cartoon *Little Hiawatha*. Walt was so pleased with Thomas's work that he assigned him as one of eight artists to animate the dwarfs in *Snow White and the Seven Dwarfs*.

While animating a scene in which Dopey was trying to catch up to the other dwarfs, Thomas added a "hitch step" to Dopey's gait. Other animators had already spent countless hours animating scenes with Dopey *without* the "hitch step." Walt liked Thomas's addition so much that he ordered all scenes with Dopey be redrawn to include the "hitch step." Several animators let Thomas know how displeased they were to have to redraw those scenes.[170]

When Walt decided to redraw Dopey's walk, *Snow White* was already way over budget. But Walt believed that by achieving the highest standards of quality, he was creating long-term value and customer loyalty. Walt's pursuit of excellence molded the culture of The Walt Disney Company and still shapes Disney values to this day.

Walt demonstrated this same obsession with quality and excellence while building Disneyland. Don Rake, a transportation engineer who worked with Roger Broggie in designing the Disneyland Railroad, recalled his first tour of the Disneyland construction site with Broggie. "As we talked and walked," Rake said, "Roger pointed to the Main Street storefronts. He explained that Walt insisted on complete second story construction, no false fronts and façades, no sham in any way. He told me that all construction was a 'complete build out' with quality materials. He explained that the castle could have been built with wire mesh frame and gunite. It would have looked natural, but Walt insisted that it be made with solid limestone blocks and mortar. This tour was a real education into the goals and character of Walt Disney."

Walt was fortunate to have Roy at his side, continually making the argument for fiscal restraint. But Roy was equally fortunate to be in business with a creative genius who was 100 percent committed to quality and excellence. It took Roy's yin and Walt's yang to make the Disney company a phenomenal success—and Roy knew it. In an essay for *Readers Digest*, February 1969, Roy reflected on the life of his late great "kid brother":

Walt was a complex man. To the writers, producers, and animators who worked with him, he was a genius who had an uncanny ability to add an extra fillip of imagination to any story or idea. To the millions of people who watched his TV show, he was a warm, kindly personality, bringing fun and pleasure into their homes.

To the bankers who financed us, I'm sure he seemed like a wild man, hell-bent for bankruptcy. To me, he was my amazing kid brother, full of impractical dreams that he made come true.[171]

Ward Kimball explained Walt's view of money: "If you want to know the real secret of Walt's success, it's that he never tried to make money. He was always trying to make something that he could have fun with or be proud of."[172] In other words, Walt was quality-conscious, not cost-conscious.

Film producer and Disney historian Les Perkins told me a story from Disneyland's first year of operation. Walt wanted to hold a twice-daily Christmas parade from late November till Christmas Day—a $350,000 extravagance.

"Walt called accountants 'bean counters,'" Perkins said. "The 'bean counters' told Walt, 'Why spend money on a Christmas parade? It won't draw people to the park. The people will already be here, so it's just an expense that we can do without. No one will complain if we dispense with the parade, because nobody's expecting it.'

"Walt said, 'That's just the point. We should do the parade precisely *because* no one's expecting it. Our goal at Disneyland is to always give the people *more* than they expect. As long as we keep surprising them, they'll keep coming back. But if they ever stop coming, it'll cost us ten times that much to get them back."

The *Long Beach Independent* reported that the first Disneyland Christmas parade, held on Thanksgiving Day 1955, was a circus parade, promoting Disneyland's Mickey Mouse Club Circus. The parade was led by grand marshals Walt Disney and Fess Parker on horseback. Fess Parker wore buckskins and a coonskin cap as Davy Crockett. Their horses were decked out with sparkling silver saddles, bridles, and reins. Behind the grand marshals came Jimmy Dodd, dressed in a ringmaster's top hat and tails, accompanied by the merry Mouseketeers. Roy Williams, "the Big Mooseketeer," sat in a carriage, dashing off quick cartoons of Mickey Mouse and handing them out to fans along Main Street.

Marching bands from around Southern California performed, along with the sixteen-piece Disneyland Band led by Disney composer Vesey Walker. Between the bands were circus acts—Bob-O the Clown, trick riders, a dog and pony act, musical seals, llamas, camels, and elephants. The Keystone Kops, Serenada the Musical Horse, the Ted DeWayne Acrobats, and an old-fashioned steam calliope brought up the rear.

The Christmas Parade began at Town Square, proceeded down Main Street, went around the Central Plaza, then passed through Frontierland. The parade's destination was Holidayland, a nine-acre section on Disneyland's western edge (near present-day New Orleans Square).[173] There, in a candy-striped big-top tent, Jimmy Dodd emceed the first Mickey Mouse Club Circus, and the Mouseketeers performed daring feats of gymnastics and acrobatics.

Mouseketeer Bobby Burgess recalled that the Mickey Mouse Club Circus was a fast-paced seventy-five-minute show. "It was hot and sweaty in there but we were having a blast. . . .We did the trapeze act.... The boys were [dressed as] Peter Pan and the girls were [dressed as] Tinker Bell and then we turned out the lights and we glowed in the dark. We also rode elephants and horses every day, and we were trained by professional circus people. That was really fun!"[174]

The Mickey Mouse Club Circus ended forever on January 8, 1956. But the Disneyland Christmas parades have been held annually since 1955. Walt insisted on it. He was committed to giving his guests more entertainment than they expected. He was quality-conscious, not cost-conscious, and his commitment to quality in every detail was one of the keys to Walt's competence as a leader.

What can we learn about leadership competence from the life of Walt Disney? Here are some of the lessons I've found by studying his life:

1. **Commit yourself to a lifetime of continuous learning.** Leaders are readers. Walt's mother taught him how to read before he started school, and he remained a voracious reader throughout his life. In 1953, one of Walt's associates at the Burbank studio told columnist Hedda Hopper, "I don't know when he finds time to read; but the extent of his knowledge is incredible. He can talk on any subject under the sun. Any child can understand him and yet I've heard him discuss splitting the atom with [Nobel-winning physicist] Dr. Robert Millikan."[175]

2. **Cultivate an enthusiasm for ideas.** Walt was a dynamo of ideas, and he surrounded himself with creative people whose imaginations roamed freely in all directions. Walt placed no limits—*none*—on the range and scope of his imagination, and he constantly urged his artists and Imagineers to do the same.

To Walt, anything around you and anything that happened to you could become grist for the mill of imagination. Walt believed that creativity is a learnable skill—and he was right.

3. **Let your people know you welcome dissenting opinions.** Any organization in which people are afraid to speak their minds, candidly and respectfully, is a dysfunctional organization. Walt had no use for yes-men. He welcomed dissent. Yes, he could be hard on new ideas, especially if they ran counter to his own views. But he wanted to hear them, and he always considered them—and sometimes he changed his mind. That's what competent leaders do.

4. **Be quality-conscious, not cost-conscious.** When a leader values excellence over profits, odds are the profits will come. This doesn't mean a leader should spend recklessly. But great leaders refuse to sacrifice quality to make a few bucks more. One of Walt's friends visited him at the Burbank studio. As they chatted, the friend said, "Walt, what do you do with all your money?" Walt pointed out the window at the studio buildings and said, "I fertilize that field with it."[176] In other words, he invested his money in improving the quality of his motion pictures. Take care of the quality, and the profits will take care of themselves.

During the 1940s, Walt coined the term "plussing," turning the conjunction "plus" into a verb, "to plus something." To plus a movie or a theme park is to improve the experience. Plussing is the act of giving your customers more than they expect, more than you are required to give, and more than they paid for. Walt plussed Mickey Mouse with sound. He plussed the Silly Symphonies with color. He plussed *Fantasia* with Fantasound. He plussed the skills of his artists, spending hundreds of thousands of dollars on art classes. He plussed Disneyland in every conceivable way.

"Disneyland is something that will never be finished," Walt once said. "It's something I can keep developing, keep plussing and adding to. It will be a living, breathing thing that will always be changing. Not only can I add new things, but even the trees will keep growing. Disneyland will get more beautiful every year."[177]

If you understand Walt's drive to plus everything he touched, then you have the key to his amazing success as a leader—and you're almost ready to lead like Walt.

7

Walt's Boldness

THROUGHOUT HIS CAREER, Walt lived courageously and led boldly, and the most challenging goal he ever attempted was Disneyland. The earliest public notice about Disneyland was probably this brief item in Danton Walker's "Broadway" column in the *New York Daily News*, January 11, 1954:

> Walt Disney is building an amusement park for kids in Los Angeles, the largest in the country, which will take two years to complete. One of the features will be the "space" section (space ships taking off to the moon, etc.).[178]

In mid-March 1954, John Lester's syndicated "Radio and Television" column stated that "Walt Disney's $10,000,000 amusement park" was already "being built in Hollywood."[179]

Of course, in March 1954, the Disney company wasn't building Disneyland in Los Angeles or Hollywood or anywhere else. Perhaps the Disney company wanted the public to *think* the new theme park would be located in or near Los Angeles. Meanwhile, Walt's representatives were quietly buying up seventeen parcels of farmland thirty-five miles south of L.A., a total of 160 acres, mostly orange groves.

"The land cost a million dollars," Walt later told UPI columnist Aline Mosby, "and getting that was the toughest job. The Stanford Research Institute surveyed the area and selected Anaheim as best. We found one tract there but when people found out what it was for, the price went up. So we found another section." Walt added that his representatives had to contact landowners as far away as Ohio to secure the real estate.[180]

There is some confusion about the date when construction of Disneyland began. An article posted at the website of D23, The Official Disney Fan Club, says that "workers began construction" of Disneyland on July 21, 1954, which would mean that Disneyland was built in less than a year.[181] But what does that date refer to? The day bulldozers began uprooting the orange groves? The day of groundbreaking? The day of pouring concrete foundations? The article doesn't say.

Neal Gabler, on page 524 of *Walt Disney: The Triumph of the American Imagination*, states that groundbreaking took place on July 12, 1954, a date I have found in no other source. Journalist Bob Thomas interviewed Walt numerous times and reported on the progress of Disneyland's construction for the Associated Press, but in two books (*Walt Disney: An American Original*, page 253, and *Building a Company: Roy O. Disney and the Creation of an Entertainment Empire*, page 189), Thomas states that the first orange tree wasn't bulldozed until August 1954, eleven months before opening day—and no other source I've seen claims construction began as late as August.

As near as I've been able to determine, construction of Disneyland officially began on Friday, July 16, 1954—exactly a year and a day before Walt's projected opening day. That's the day crews began surveying the land and clearing orange trees. There was apparently no official ground-breaking ceremony, but on Wednesday, July 21, 1954, construction crews unofficially broke ground to begin re-contouring the land—leveling ground, building berms, digging moats and riverbeds (this is the date given by D23). On Friday, August 13, 1954, crews began removing the nearly twenty farm houses, barns, and other buildings that stood on the property—and this may be why Bob Thomas listed August as the month construction began.

I believe that, in Walt's mind, construction began the day his crews first set foot on the property with their survey stakes, theodolites, and instrument stands to measure his kingdom. Walt deliberately gave himself a deadline of a year and a day to build his kingdom, from July 16, 1954 to July 17, 1955. Peggy Matthews Rose, a longtime Disney cast member and Disney authority who assisted us on *How to Be Like Walt*, told me that when she worked for Disney in the 1970s, people often spoke of Disneyland as being built in "a year and a day."

Walt gave himself four years to build New Orleans Square, a mere three-acre section of Disneyland. Yet he set a seemingly impossible goal of building all 160 acres of Disneyland, with all its elaborate attractions, in just a year and a day. We must wonder why Walt set such a tight deadline for himself. My writing partner, Jim Denney, researched this question and came up with a fascinating theory that is closely tied to Walt's unique capacity for bold, visionary leadership.

"It occurred to me," Jim said, "that the time frame Walt chose—a year and a day—might be especially significant to him. We know that symbols were important to Walt, not because he was superstitious but because they had sentimental meaning to him. For example, he went to the City of Anaheim and specifically requested the street address 1313 S. Harbor Boulevard for Disneyland because the thirteenth letter of the alphabet is M. Whose initials are MM or '13–13'? Mickey Mouse, of course."

In his research, Jim found a newspaper column by United Press writer Aline Mosby from May 1954, two months before construction began on Disneyland. She had interviewed Walt and had viewed the plans for Disneyland at the Burbank studio. "An eighty-foot high King Arthur castle will be built in the 'fantasy' section of Disneyland," she wrote.

That's right. Walt was not planning to call it Sleeping Beauty Castle in early 1954. He was calling it "King Arthur Castle." And as you walk through Sleeping Beauty Castle today, what is the first thing you see in the courtyard beyond? King Arthur's Carrousel. In 1954, Walt planned for much of Fantasyland to have a King Arthur theme. Why? Because the stories of King Arthur had impacted him deeply in his boyhood. All of Disneyland was a re-creation of Walt's most treasured boyhood memories, and his fascination with King Arthur and his Knights of the Round Table is on full display in Fantasyland.

What does King Arthur have to do with Walt's goal of building Disneyland in a year and a day? Simply this: A year and a day was a significant period of time in Arthurian legend. An Arthurian tale called *The Hanes Taliesin* tells of a magical cauldron that boiled for a year and a day. In another Arthurian tale, *Sir Gawain and the Green Knight*, the Green Knight vows to return and strike Sir Gawain with an axe in a year and a day. In Thomas Malory's novel *Le Morte d'Arthur*, Sir Gawain swears an oath to go in quest of the Holy Grail and not return to Camelot for a year and a day. And even Mark Twain, in *A Connecticut Yankee in King Arthur's Court*, pays homage to that tradition when he writes of three knights going off to seek adventures, and not returning for "a year and a day—and without baggage."[182]

"I'm convinced," Jim told me, "that Walt saw Disneyland as his Holy Grail. From boyhood to manhood, he pursued this bold quest. I think he deliberately chose the Arthurian time frame as an incentive to complete his quest on time. And it worked. I can't prove that all of that was in Walt's mind, but I believe it to be true."

On July 17, 1955, the gates of Walt's kingdom opened, and there was his shining grail. Like a knight of the Round Table, Sir Walter of Marceline completed his quest and turned his bold vision into reality—and he accomplished it all in a year and a day.

Courage to Step Off the Path

I define boldness as courage, confidence, an adventurous spirit. Boldness is an eagerness to accept tough challenges and take risks to achieve great goals. Boldness does not mean fearlessness. Bold leaders know fear, but they have mastered their fears and dare to do the very thing that makes them afraid. Bold leaders also accept the consequences of their actions and decisions.

Walt was one of the boldest leaders in American business history. More than once, he bet everything he had—from his studio to his life insurance policy—on a single project. He said, "Courage is the main quality of leadership, in my opinion, no matter where it is exercised. Usually it implies some risk—especially in new undertakings. Courage to initiate something and to keep it going."[183]

He encouraged this same adventurous spirit in the people who worked for him. Wendell Warner, a former engineer at the Burbank studio, told me, "Walt expected his people to take a chance and fly high. If you failed, you'd better not shift the blame to others. Walt was never easygoing about failure. But if you took a chance and failed, he wouldn't fire you or berate you. He wanted you to learn and grow from the experience.

"There were times when I made a mistake on some project, and I'd go to Walt and say, 'I blew it. I tried to pull something off, and I failed.' Walt would say, 'Well, did you learn anything?' And I'd say, 'Yes, absolutely.' And Walt would say, 'Okay, then it's not a total loss, is it? Keep trying—and keep an eye on what other people are doing around the shop. See what you can learn from them.'... Walt always made you feel that failure could be redeemed, and he expected you to continue working and risking until you achieved success."

Tom Nabbe began working at Disneyland on opening day, July 17, 1955. He was twelve years old, and he walked up and down Main Street selling the park's daily newspaper, *The Disneyland News*. The young Disneyland newsboy impressed Walt with his bold enthusiasm. Tom would often go to the waterfront of the Rivers of America and watch construction work on Tom Sawyer Island. Whenever Tom saw Walt at the park, he'd walk right up and ask Walt to hire him to play the part of Tom Sawyer.

The first time Tom asked, Walt responded, "Why should I put you on the island when I can put a mannequin there?"

But Tom wouldn't take no for an answer. He pursued Walt again and again for the better part of a year—and Walt must have admired Tom's boldness.

A few weeks before Tom Sawyer Island opened in June 1956, Tom was playing pinball in one of the park's arcades. Dick Nunis, then the supervisor of Frontierland, walked up and said, "Tom, come with me."

Leaving his pinball game unfinished, Tom followed Nunis to the Rivers of America. Walt was there, talking to his landscaper, Morgan "Bill" Evans, about Tom Sawyer Island. Dick said, "Here's Tom."

Walt turned to the boy and said, "Are you still interested in working here as Tom Sawyer?"

Tom's eyes lit up. "You bet!"

And just like that, Tom Nabbe became Tom Sawyer. Walt explained that Tom needed a work permit and Social Security card to play the role (they hadn't been required for his newsboy job).

Once Tom got his paperwork in order, he went to the Disneyland employment office and asked for the employment forms. He told the woman at the desk that Walt had hired him to play Tom Sawyer. The woman called her supervisor over and told him the situation. The supervisor turned to Tom and said flatly that Walt Disney did not hire kids.

"Call Dick Nunis," Tom said. "He'll tell you that Walt hired me."

The supervisor called Nunis—then he gave Tom the employment forms to fill out. Tom was officially hired as a Disneyland cast member with the title of Guest Relations Assistant, earning the princely wage of 75 cents an hour.

Walt required Tom to maintain a minimum of a C average in school. Every quarter, Tom showed his report card personally to Walt. In the summertime, Tom worked five days a week, nine a.m. to five-thirty p.m. He worked only on weekends during the school year.

Every few weeks, Walt would sit down with Tom and ask questions about his role as Tom Sawyer, his interactions with guests, and any ideas he had for improving the island. Tom Nabbe gave Walt two ideas that were implemented on the island—the addition of Tom and Huck's Treehouse and the addition of a "secret" escape tunnel in Fort Wilderness.

During his years in the Tom Sawyer role, Tom Nabbe talked to countless guests, both young and old. He answered thousands of questions (in character as Tom Sawyer) and posed for photos with Disneyland guests. His job also entailed setting out fishing poles, baiting fish hooks with worms, and cleaning any fish the guests caught (for a time, during Disneyland's first few years, the waters around Tom Sawyer Island were stocked with bluegills and catfish).[184]

Tom Nabbe told me about a conversation he once had with Walt—a conversation about courage and boldness. "One day," Tom said, "I was walking to Tom Sawyer Island with Walt. He said, 'Tom, there are paths on that island, but those paths are really for the moms and dads. I want young people to make their own paths and explore the island in their own way.'

"I've often thought about what Walt was really telling me. He wasn't just talking about that island. He was talking about life. Walt was saying that we all need to approach life creatively and courageously. We shouldn't just stick to the paths that are laid out for us. We need to explore. It takes courage to step off the path and blaze a new trail, but that's what creativity is all about. Walt really believed that. What's more, he lived it."

In 1961, Tom aged out of the Tom Sawyer role. Walt found him another job working with Disneyland attractions. Another young man played the part of Tom Sawyer that summer, but the new boy left in the fall and Walt never hired another Tom Sawyer. Tom Nabbe went on to spend his entire career with Disney and later helped to open Walt Disney World in Florida as the Monorail supervisor. He retired from Disney in 2003 and was named a Disney Legend with his own window on Main Street in Walt Disney World's Magic Kingdom. Known as "The Luckiest Boy in the World," Tom Nabbe chronicled his Disneyland career in *From Disneyland's Tom Sawyer to Disney Legend: The Adventures of Tom Nabbe.*

Tom's story teaches us to live boldly, to pursue your goals boldly, and to never be afraid to ask the boss for that dream job. I think Walt must have recognized a bit of his own early boldness in young Tom Nabbe—and he wanted to encourage the boy's spirit of adventure. Like Tom Nabbe, we need to hear what Walt is saying to us about boldness and courage. If we are not bold, if we are not living the adventure, then we are not leading.

Encouraging a Culture of Boldness

Walt not only exhibited bold leadership and respected boldness in the people who worked for him, but he encouraged a culture of bold risk-taking and can-do confidence throughout his organization. As a result, the boldly uninhibited Rolly Crump became one of Walt's favorite artists for any project calling for a wildly innovative approach.

One day Walt called a meeting of his top Imagineers and announced, "We're making some changes to Adventureland, and I think I'd like to put a Tiki Room there.... I want it to be a restaurant."

He explained his concept of the Enchanted Tiki Room Restaurant (though he would later abandon the restaurant concept and turn the Enchanted Tiki Room into Disneyland's first Audio-Animatronics show). Walt named John Hench as lead artist for the Tiki Room interior and assigned Rolly Crump to design the exterior waiting area. "Rolly," Walt said, "we can't have people waiting outside the Tiki Room with nothing to see, and so I want you to design a pre-show. Let's have the show feature Tiki gods."

Rolly knew little about the Polynesian culture on which the Tiki theme is based. So he went to the public library and returned with an armload of books about Polynesian religion and folklore. Using pictures in the books for reference, he began sketching Polynesian idols. His sketches of Hina, the goddess of mist and rain, and Pele, the goddess of volcanoes and fire, were faithful to the photos he found in the books. But he wasn't content to simply copy the idols he found in books. He decided to invent one idol with an extra dash of Disney magic.

Rolly had heard that Chinese farmers used an ingenious device that used dripping water to generate a clacking sound to keep small animals out of their gardens. Rolly designed an idol that incorporated this device to produce sound and motion. The idol would spit water into a bamboo tube. As the tube filled with water, it would tip, dump the water, swing back up, and make a loud *clack* by striking a wooden peg. Rolly knew that Walt was a stickler for authenticity and that there were no idols with moving parts or running water in Polynesian culture—yet he couldn't resist the notion of a Tiki idol that spits and clacks.

John Hench and Rolly Crump presented their sketches to Walt and anxiously awaited his verdict. Walt looked at the sketches in silence for a long time. Finally, Walt said, "Are these sketches authentic?"

Both men assured Walt that the Tiki sketches were "authentic." Their assurances were technically true. So-called "Tiki culture" is a style of décor loosely based on Polynesian culture, but with its origins in California in the 1930s. So Rolly's spitting, clacking Tiki idol was no less "authentic" than any other Tiki-style statue—even though it's unlikely such an idol ever existed on any Polynesian island.

Walt pointed to the spitting god with the bamboo device and asked, "What's he the god of?"

Hench knew that Rolly hadn't given the spitting idol a name, so he spoke up and said, "That's the god of tapa cloth beating." Tapa is a colorful Polynesian cloth made by beating the bark of the paper mulberry tree with wooden mallets. To Hench, the clacking of the bamboo suggested the beating of the tapa cloth.[185]

But Walt misheard Hench's explanation. He thought Hench had said, "That's the god of the tapa clock beating."

Walt said, "Clock?"

Nodding (and without missing a beat), Hench said, "It's the god that tells the time."

Walt continued to mull the drawing in silence. Finally, he said, "Okay, then.... Build him."

Rolly knew that Walt would eventually want to know the name of the Polynesian god of time. So Rolly went home to his books, hoping to find that there was, in truth, a time god among the Polynesians. And there was. His name was Maui. Problem solved.

But Rolly had another problem: Walt had told him to "build" the Polynesian god of time—in other words, Walt expected Rolly to sculpt Maui out of clay. But Rolly had never sculpted anything in his life. He had always worked in two dimensions, not three.

So Rolly took the sketches to Blaine Gibson, the studio sculptor, and told him what Walt wanted.

"I'm too busy, Rolly," Gibson said. "I can't do it."

"So who else is around to sculpt them?"

"You are."

Having no choice, Rolly made up his mind to learn how to sculpt. There was no time to take sculpting classes. He had to learn by doing.

Gibson gave him a quick-start explanation of how to make an armature (the wire skeleton of the sculpture) and how to apply the clay to the armature. Gibson also told Rolly where to get the plasticine clay for sculpting. Plasticine is hard when cold, but moldable when warm, so Rolly did his sculpting in the studio parking lot, where the Burbank sunshine kept the clay warm and pliable. His sculpting tool was a plastic fork he took from the studio commissary. The first piece Rolly sculpted was Maui, the spitting, clacking time god. It turned out just like his drawing. So he proceeded to sculpt the other idols.

The studio fabricating shop made molds of Rolly's hand-sculpted statues and then cast the idols in fiberglass. Rolly hand-painted the fiberglass sculptures and installed them himself in the Tiki Room forecourt, bolting them into place. The idols of Maui and the rest of Rolly's Pacific island pantheon are still on display at Walt Disney's Enchanted Tiki Room in Disneyland. Idols cast from Rolly's original sculptures have also been added to Disney's Polynesian Village in Florida and the Tahitian Terrace restaurant at Hong Kong Disneyland. The sign next to Rolly's creation reads:

MAUI

Who roped the playful sun
Through his special mystic powers
He made the sun keep regular hours
Maui tells us time to go
Time for wondrous Tiki show

Rolly concluded, "Today, such a project would involve dozens of people, reams of paperwork, and hours of planning. Back then, we just did things. If we didn't know how to do them, we figured them out, then did them. I think, doing it our way, we got much more done. It was marvelous!"[186]

To give you an idea of how bold Rolly Crump was, let me tell you one more story. While sculpting Tiki gods in the studio parking lot, Rolly would hop on his motorcycle during lunch breaks and ride around the lot. One day, a studio secretary approached him as he was parking his cycle. She said she had never ridden a motorcycle before.

"Get on back," Rolly said. "Where's your desk?" She got on and gave him directions to the building where she worked.

Rolly revved his engine and took off. He drove the secretary to her building, through the open front door, down the wide corridor, and right to the office where she worked—next door to the office of Dick Irvine, who was in charge of Disneyland attractions. As the secretary hopped off the idling motorcycle, Dick Irvine opened his office door and peered out.

"Oh," Irvine said with a shrug, "it's just Rolly." Then he ducked inside and closed the door. Rolly rode out of the building the same way he'd ridden in.[187]

Why did Walt and his associates encourage this wildly creative genius, Rolly Crump? They knew that the same impetuous boldness that prompted him to ride a motorcycle through an office building also left its imprint on many Disney animated films and such Disneyland attractions as "it's a small world," The Haunted Mansion, and the Enchanted Tiki Room. Walt didn't want to do anything to inhibit Rolly's bold creativity.

Throughout his years of leadership, Walt encouraged a culture of boldness. Walt wasn't interested in excuses, such as, "I've never done that before." Walt *specialized* in doing what had never been done before, so he expected his people to demonstrate a bold and adventuresome spirit—and they rarely disappointed him.

Learning to Lead Boldly

In 1935, the League of Nations invited Walt to Paris. The League wished to honor Walt for promoting global goodwill through his beloved Mickey Mouse cartoons. At the time, his studio was one year into production of *Snow White and the Seven Dwarfs*, and Walt was reluctant to be away from the studio.

Roy reminded Walt that 1935 marked the ten-year wedding anniversary for Walt and Lillian and for Roy and Edna. The Disney couples could enjoy a second honeymoon in Europe—and Walt could visit European castles as research for *Snow White*. The latter argument persuaded Walt.

They toured England, France, Holland, Switzerland, and Italy. In England, Walt was introduced to H. G. Wells and the royal family. In Italy, he met the pope. But the highlight of the tour occurred in Paris, when Walt came upon a theater that was running *eight* Disney cartoons back-to-back without a feature film. Here was proof that audiences would eagerly sit for an hour or more of non-stop Disney animation. Walt knew he was on the right track in making *Snow White*.

Walt boldly bet everything he had on one motion picture—and his bet paid off beyond his wildest dreams. Where does this kind of leadership boldness come from? Where do we find the courage to live and lead boldly?

Few people are born with fearless self-confidence. Most of us must learn boldness by taking on challenges that seem too big for us. Sometimes we'll fail, just as Walt failed when his Kansas City animation studio went bankrupt and when his animators abandoned him and he lost control of Oswald the Lucky Rabbit. Walt failed—then he picked himself up, dusted himself off, and discovered that he still had his health, his ideas, and his boldness. He learned that failure is nothing but a lesson to be learned along the path to success.

On October 1, 1966, Walt delivered one of the last speeches of his career when he accepted the Showman of the World Award from the National Association of Theater Owners. In that speech, delivered at New York's Americana Hotel just two and a half months before his death, Walt briefly surveyed his career. The tone of Walt's speech was characteristically humble and self-effacing, but the leadership trait that shines through Walt's words is his boldness. Here are some highlights from that speech:

I propose to go backwards—almost forty-five years ago to Kansas City, Missouri....I was all alone then. I didn't even have a mouse. But I had some ideas....I packed all of my worldly goods in a pasteboard suitcase, and with that wonderful audacity of youth, I went to Hollywood—arriving there with just $40 as my total cash assets....

My big brother, Roy, was already in Los Angeles as a patient in the Veteran's Hospital. When he got out, we had more in common than brotherly love. Both of us were unemployed—and neither could get a job. We solved the problem by going into business ourselves. We established the first animated cartoon studio in Hollywood.

Several years after producing one series after another on a shoestring budget...Mickey Mouse came into our life. At first, it looked like he was going to have a harder time crashing show business than I had. Nobody wanted Mickey....

At the time we were in desperate need for $500. To put it briefly, everything owned by Roy and me was mortgaged to the hilt. So I asked Harry [Reichenbach, manager of the Old Colony Theatre on Broadway] for $500 for exhibiting the first Mickey Mouse one week....He said,

"Let's compromise. I'll give you $250 a week—and run the cartoon for two weeks." ... Harry sold the public Mickey Mouse in just two weeks. Our red ink took on a blacker hue. . . .

With the success of Mickey, I was determined to diversify. I had another idea which was plaguing my brain. It was The Silly Symphonies. A series without a central character which would give me latitude to develop the animated cartoon medium. The first was *The Skeleton Dance*. The reaction was, "Why does Walt fool around with skeletons? Give us more mice."

So, for a while, it looked like the first Silly Symphony would not get out of the graveyard. But once more, a showman came to the rescue. Fred Miller, who was managing director of the Carthay Circle Theatre in Los Angeles, took a chance on the film.

The Skeleton Dance got a wonderful reception, and wonderful reviews. ... The success of The Silly Symphonies gave us the courage for *Snow White*. And you should have heard the howls of warning! It was prophesied that nobody would sit through a cartoon an hour and a half long.

But we had decided there was only one way we could successfully do *Snow White*—and that was to go for broke—shoot the works. There would be no compromise on money, talent, or time. We did not know whether the public would go for a cartoon feature; but we were darned sure that audiences would not buy a bad cartoon feature.

As the *Snow White* budget climbed, I did begin to wonder whether we would ever get our investment back. ... Then came a shocker. Roy told me that we would have to borrow another quarter of a million dollars to finish the movie. "You've got to show the bankers what's been completed on *Snow White* as collateral." I had always objected to letting any outsider see an incomplete motion picture.

I had to sit alone with Joe Rosenberg of the Bank of America and try to sell him a quarter of a million dollars' worth of faith. He showed not the slightest reaction to what he viewed. After the lights came on he walked out of the projection room, remarked that it was a nice day—and yawned! He was still deadpan as I conducted him to his car. Then he turned to me and said, "Walt, that picture will make a pot full of money." To this day, he's my favorite banker.[188]

Do you see the progression of Walt's leadership career—and the steady growth of his confidence and boldness? The success of Mickey Mouse gave him the courage to diversify and create the Silly Symphonies. The success of the Silly Symphonies gave him the courage to take on the challenge of *Snow White and the Seven Dwarfs*. And the success of *Snow White* led to even greater challenges. Some succeeded. Some flopped. But his confidence and his boldness continued to grow as his goals became steadily bigger and more challenging.

It's instructive to note that, even before *Snow White* was completed, Walt was already planning three new feature-length fully animated motion pictures: *Pinocchio, Bambi*, and *Fantasia*. He was confident that if he could see *Snow White* through to completion, it was going to completely change his business model. His confidence was justified. As Walt recalled, "When *Snow White* hit, we realized we were in a new business. We knew it within a week after the picture had opened at the Carthay Circle in Los Angeles. We had been heavily in debt and within six months we had millions in the bank."[189]

From the day *Snow White* premiered, the Disney studio ceased to be merely a cartoon factory. It had become a feature-length motion picture studio. And in the process, Walt had changed the course of animation history.

THE BOLDNESS TO BUILD MOUNTAINS

During the construction of Disneyland, workers dug up tons of dirt to form the channels of the Rivers of America and the Sleeping Beauty Castle moat. They trucked those masses of dirt to a location on the border between Fantasyland and Tomorrowland. The result was an unsightly hill about twenty feet in height. Walt wasn't sure what to do with that hill, so he had his master botanist, Morgan "Bill" Evans, plant shrubs and grass on it to make it less of an eyesore. Then he had it fenced off so that no one would climb the hill and get hurt. (The fence, however, proved to be only a minor obstacle to couples who sneaked onto the hill and used it as a lovers' lane.)

That dirt pile was known by various names but was most commonly called Holiday Hill. Something about Holiday Hill reminded Walt of snowy winters when he was a boy in Marceline. As he recalled in a letter to the *Marceline News*, published September 2, 1938, "What fun I used to have on winter days going down the hillsides lickety-split on a sled."[190]

So Walt proposed bringing in a powerful snow-making machine to blizzard the hill with snow, and then providing Disneyland guests with year-round toboggan rides. Walt's horrified construction boss, Admiral Joe Fowler, pointed out that California summers would quickly turn all that snow into a torrential run-off. Walt reluctantly agreed that the toboggan idea was impractical.

Walt also decided that the notion of a twenty-foot hill with toboggan rides was not a bold enough idea. He needed to envision something much bigger, much bolder, much more challenging—but what? The shrub-covered hill nagged at him during Disneyland's first few years.

One day in 1957 or 1958, a Disneyland cast member noticed Walt sitting on a park bench in Central Plaza. He was gazing off toward a patch of empty sky between Sleeping Beauty Castle and the Monsanto House of the Future. The cast member said, "What are you looking at, Walt?"

Pointing off toward that empty sky, Walt said, "My mountain."

There was no mountain there—but Walt saw it nonetheless. It was a big enough, bold enough vision to be worthy of Walt and his Disneyland. Forgotten was the vision of a twenty-foot-high dirt hill with snow and toboggans. In its place stood a towering mountain, 147 feet high, with two intertwined steel roller coaster tracks, ice caves, waterfalls, and thrilling splashdown pools.

As he stared into that empty space, envisioning his mountain, he probably didn't know what shape it would take. He didn't specifically envision the Matterhorn. Those details would be filled in during the summer of 1958, when Walt was in the Swiss village of Zermatt. There he first laid eyes on the Matterhorn—and he couldn't take his eyes off it. His vision for his Disneyland mountain was complete at last.

It was an incredibly bold idea. At first his Imagineers doubted it could even be built. Imagineer Harriet Burns thought the Matterhorn project was "crazy." Walt was trying to cram too many features into the non-geometrical shape of the Matterhorn. "Nothing like the Matterhorn had ever been built before," she recalled. "Walt would bring in experts and engineers to advise him on the problems we were likely to encounter. He always wanted the very best advice he could get. But if the experts said, 'This is impossible, this can't be done,' it rolled right off of him.... He had accomplished the so-called 'impossible' so many times in his life that the word no longer had any meaning to him."[191]

The Matterhorn Bobsleds opened on June 14, 1959. It's a Walt Disney original—no other Disney theme park in the world has a Matterhorn attraction (though Disney's Animal Kingdom in Florida now has a 199-foot-tall Expedition Everest attraction, inspired by Disneyland's Matterhorn). Walt's mountain defines the Disneyland skyline to this day, and it stands as a monument to the boldness of Walt's leadership.

What can we learn about bold, courageous leadership from Walt's life? Let me suggest three key lessons:

1. **Cultivate a spirit of adventure in your leadership life.** Commit yourself to a leadership style based on bold decision making, a confident communication style, and setting challenging goals. Take risks—not wild, foolish, reckless gambles, but calculated risks. Start small and build up to bigger and riskier challenges. Sure, you'll feel afraid at times. You'll doubt yourself now and then. Just keep moving forward, keep stepping away from the path, keep blazing a bold trail through the leadership wilderness. Dare to astonish the world.

2. **Encourage a culture of boldness in your team or organization.** Reward and applaud the bold risk-takers on your team. When they succeed, recognize their accomplishments in front of the entire team. When they fail, applaud their bold attempts and tell them to keep trying. If you punish failure, you'll inhibit their courage and confidence—and you'll stifle their boldness. Innovation and creativity are by-products of boldness. So encourage your people. Believe in them. Build their confidence and reward their boldness.

3. **Keep upping the ante.** Every time we take on a challenge that's too big for us and we succeed, our courage ratchets up a notch.

Our confidence grows so we can dare to attempt even greater things. Film historian J. B. Kaufman (coauthor, with Russell Merritt, of *Walt in Wonderland*) told me, "Walt started with small goals—first, a little studio in Kansas City, then a bigger one in Hollywood, then a massive studio in Burbank, then a theme park in Anaheim, then an entire city in Florida. Each goal was a big one at the time, but once he accomplished it, he would get restless and he would want to go beyond it, to something bigger and more daring. He was not just a man of ideas. He was a man of daring and courage."

When you look to the horizons of your life, what do you see? A little dirt hill—or a mountain of a thrill ride? Is your vision bold enough? Are your sights set high enough? Check your pulse—is your heart beating faster? Are you feeling a tingle of fear and excitement and eagerness to scale new heights?

Do you have the boldness to lead like Walt?

8

Walt's Serving Heart

HAVE YOU HEARD OF WALT'S "lost" Disney theme park?

It wasn't going to be located in California or Florida. It was planned for the state of Missouri. Walt had his Imagineers draw renderings, elevations, and site maps. He purchased 200 acres of property (forty more acres than Disneyland) and had optioned an additional 500 acres through his holding company, Retlaw Enterprises. He was eager to start building his Missouri theme park when doctors told him he was dying of cancer. Knowing his time was short, Walt asked Roy to see his Missouri theme park through to completion—but the daunting Florida project kept Roy occupied until his own death in December 1971.

Walt called his "lost" theme park The Marceline Project, and he planned to present it as a gift to the town where he had spent his earliest, happiest years. Walt had big plans for his Marceline theme park. It would have been reminiscent of the Henry Ford Museum and Greenfield Village in Michigan, but with a more rural and small-town theme. The Walt Disney Hometown Museum, located in the restored Santa Fe Railroad Depot in Marceline, contains the plans and drawings Walt had prepared for his Marceline theme park.

The park would have featured such attractions as a barn dance, a fishing lake, a village similar to Main Street USA with a hotel, barber shop, general store, butcher shop, an old-time service station, and much more. Walt even planned to re-create the coal mine where, in the wintertime, he sledded down a snow-capped hill of mine tailings. He wanted Bob Gurr to design a fleet of old-fashioned vehicles like those at Disneyland—plus he planned to have an old-fashioned steam train (of course) and other attractions.

The centerpiece of The Marceline Project would have been the forty-five-acre Disney family farm. That was where Walt's childhood dreams were born, and Walt wanted to preserve the place as a "living history farm." He had conducted feasibility studies for the project, and the governor of Missouri had committed to building a four-lane highway to Marceline.

When Walt died, all those splendid plans were shelved. Walt's friends, Inez and Rush Johnson, bought the forty-acre original Disney farm to preserve the landmarks of Walt's childhood—the farmhouse, the barn, and the ancient cottonwood tree called "the Dreaming Tree." Retlaw Enterprises sold off the rest of the property Walt had acquired. The Marceline Project passed into history, unbuilt and largely forgotten.[192]

Walt had already paid tribute to his beloved hometown in many ways. He evoked his nostalgia for Marceline in such films as *So Dear to My Heart* and *Lady and the Tramp*. Disneyland's Main Street USA is an idealized version of Marceline. In fact, just off of Main Street, around the corner from the Market House, stands a façade marked "Hotel Marceline." But Walt had a serving heart. He wanted to do more than merely honor his beloved hometown from afar. He wanted to serve Marceline and thank the town for giving him the happiest years of his life. He would have achieved his goal if he'd had more time.

The ultimate test of leadership is this: Does the leader have the heart of a servant? Walt Disney led by serving.

Just a Farm Boy from Marceline

Decades after he left his beloved home town, Walt reconnected with Marceline—because of a swimming pool.

In 1955, the people of Marceline voted for a bond issue to build a community swimming pool. Rush Johnson was a city council member at the time, and he proposed that the city seek Walt's permission to name the community pool in his honor. Other members of the council were skeptical. Walt had only lived in Marceline for five years, they said. He was just a little boy when he left. He probably didn't even remember the town.

But Rush Johnson wrote to Walt, and Walt eagerly replied, "I have nothing but good memories of Marceline. It would be an honor to have my name on that pool. Marceline was my only childhood."[193]

Walt and Roy, along with their wives, went to Marceline for the dedication of the pool on the Fourth of July 1956. The Disney brothers also hosted the Midwest premiere of *The Great Locomotive Chase* at Marceline's Uptown Theatre. It was a sweltering Missouri summer and the only hotel in town had no air conditioning. Rush Johnson and his wife Inez had the only air-conditioned home in Marceline, so Walt and Roy stayed as guests in their home and became well acquainted with the Johnsons. Walt remained good friends with the couple throughout the last decade of his life.

During Walt's stay in Marceline, he and Lillian visited his old elementary school, and Walt found the very desk where he had sat as a child. He identified it by the initials W.D. carved into the desktop with a penknife.[194]

Walt returned to Marceline in 1960 when the town's elementary school was named in his honor. In fact, he canceled an around-the-world trip just so he could return home to Marceline. Walt again stayed with Rush and Inez Johnson.

He had one of his top animators paint a mural featuring more than twenty Disney characters. The mural still hangs at the school today. Walt donated Disney educational books and films to the school library, and a set of the *Encyclopædia Britannica* for every classroom. He gave the school a flag pole from the 1960 Squaw Valley Olympics, which Walt had helped organize. Humble as always, he told the people of Marceline, "I'm just a farm boy from Marceline who hides behind a duck and a mouse."[195]

From 1957 to 1966, an attraction called the Midget Autopia was located in Fantasyland near where "it's a small world" stands now. When Disneyland closed the Midget Autopia, Walt had the entire ride dismantled, crated, and shipped to Marceline. The ride operated in Marceline's Walt Disney Municipal Park for eleven years. Walt had planned to take part in the dedication ceremony in July 1966 but canceled due to ill health. (This was four months before he was diagnosed with cancer.)

Walt loved the people of Marceline, and they loved him back. He had big plans for his home town, but he died too soon. On the evening of the day Walt died, CBS News commentator Eric Sevareid eulogized him, saying that Walt Disney "probably did more to heal, or at least soothe, troubled human spirits than all the psychiatrists in the world."[196] It's true. Walt was more than an entertainer. He was a healer with a serving heart.

"I Love You, Uncle Walt!"

One of my favorite leadership paradoxes is the principle which states that you cannot be a great leader unless you are a servant. Great leaders serve the people they lead. They serve the public. They serve the stakeholders and shareholders. They serve future generations. Leadership is service. You cannot lead unless you know how to serve. A leader without a serving heart is just a boss.

Art Linkletter told me about the first time he met Walt. It was 1940, and Art was a young radio broadcaster in San Francisco. Walt was in San Francisco to host the premiere of *Fantasia*. "I arrived early for the press conference," Art recalled, "and I found the place empty except for one fellow who was busily arranging chairs. I said, 'When is Walt Disney supposed to arrive?' He grinned and said, 'I'm Walt Disney.' I said, 'You are? Why are you arranging chairs?' He said, 'Well, I like to have things just-so.' That was quite an introduction, because it gave me a glimpse of the kind of person Walt was. He wasn't a Hollywood big shot, impressed with his own importance. He was just a friendly, humble guy."

A genuine leader should never be too proud to set up chairs or make coffee or sweep the floor. A leader should always be ready to serve.

Boby Williams had just graduated from Garden Grove High School in 1958 when she applied for a job at Disneyland. Early one morning, before Disneyland opened, she walked up to the front gate and told the security guard she wanted to apply for a job. The guard let her in, and she wandered around Disneyland, looking for a place to apply. In Frontierland, she got to see the sailing ship *Columbia* arrive at the dock on its maiden voyage. Then she went back to Main Street where the Ruggles China & Gifts shop had just opened its doors. In the doorway stood Phil Papel, owner of the shop. At that time, Phil and his wife Sophie rented retail space on Main Street (Disneyland owns the shop today, which is now called The China Closet).

Boby told Phil Papel she was looking for a job. As they chatted, Boby concluded, "There was no doubt—this was where I wanted to spend the rest of my life." Papel hired her, and she started the next day. She spent forty years working for the Papels, first at Disneyland, and later at the Papels' other retail shops at the Disneyland Hotel, the Movieland Wax Museum in Buena Park, and the *Queen Mary* in Long Beach.

Boby recalled that she would enter Disneyland through the cast member entrance on Harbor Boulevard and park in the employee lot behind the Main Street shops. On her way to the Ruggles shop, she would pass Disneyland's music director Vesey Walker as he assembled his Disneyland Band backstage for the morning march down Main Street. The moment she passed through the gate and stepped onto Main Street, she said, she felt "an intense, physical feeling of peace and calm that would last all day." She added that phrases used to describe Disneyland—"The Happiest Place on Earth" and "The Magic

Kingdom"—were not just words; they were true. And this spirit of happiness, she said, "was all created by Walt Disney."

Her first encounter with Walt occurred soon after she began working at the Ruggles shop. "We received a large number of boxes in our back area," Boby recalled. "Phil handed me a box cutter and asked me to open and check in the merchandise. I had never even seen a box cutter before. As I was struggling, a voice behind me said, 'Do you need some help?' I turned around and there stood Walt Disney, with a big smile on his face. He took the box cutter from me and opened every case. I thanked him and, still smiling, he turned and walked away."

Boby's next encounter with Walt came at Christmastime 1958. In the late 1950s, when many Main Street shops were independently owned and operated, Walt would personally judge the window displays and present a trophy to the store owner with the best display. For three Christmas seasons, Papel had tried and failed to win the trophy. For Christmastime 1958, he hired a professional window decorator. The decorator spent two days on the display, and Papel paid a lot of money—and after the decorator left, Phil was unhappy with the window. Phil asked Boby to see what she could do with the display, so she spent hours trying to improve it.

Finally, Walt came by and studied the Ruggles window with a keen eye. A few days later, Walt returned with a two-foot-tall inscribed trophy. Boby's display had won—and Walt's awarding of the trophy was one of the biggest thrills of her life. She fondly concluded, "I love you, Uncle Walt!"[197]

Whether he was setting up chairs for a press conference, opening merchandise cartons with a box cutter, or awarding a trophy for Main Street window displays, Walt led by serving. He had a serving heart, and he proved that the greatest leader is a servant of all.

Walt, Servant of the World

For years after Disneyland opened, Walt had been planning an attraction that would express his desire for world peace and racial harmony. But where in the park would he put it? And how would he pay for it?

In 1963, the Pepsi soft drink company asked the Disney company to design and build an attraction for the 1964 New York World's Fair. Through WED Enterprises, Disney was already building World's Fair attractions for the state of Illinois, Ford, General Electric, and Kodak. Pepsi had waited until only eleven months remained before the Fair's opening day. Pepsi executives contacted Joe Fowler, the general manager of Disneyland and its attractions, asking Disney to build a Pepsi-sponsored attraction to benefit UNICEF, the United Nations International Children's Emergency Fund. Fowler thought the deadline was impossible to meet, so he turned Pepsi down.

Actress Joan Crawford, widow of Pepsi's past president Alfred Steele and a member of the Pepsi board, went to her friend Walt Disney and asked why he had turned Pepsi down. It was the first Walt had heard of Pepsi's request—Joe Fowler hadn't mentioned it to him. Walt told Joan Crawford that Disney would build the attraction. Finally, Walt could build the attraction he had dreamed of, in which the children of the world, arrayed in vibrant ethnic costumes, would sing songs of peace and harmony. Best of all, Pepsi would foot the bill.

The working title for the attraction was Children of the World, but it would ultimately be known as "it's a small world" (the official styling of the title uses all lowercase letters). Walt saw the attraction as his gift to the world, his vision of a utopian tomorrow in which all the world's children could hold hands and sing together without fear of hunger, poverty, war, or racism.

Walt called a meeting of his top artists and Imagineers. "I've been thinking about this for quite awhile," he told them. "There's still one piece of real estate left at the World's Fair. I want to use that real estate for a little boat ride."[198]

He chose Marc Davis and his wife Alice to design the characters and costumes. Walt's resident mad genius Rolly Crump was in charge of toys and props, while Blaine Gibson would construct the dolls. Master vehicle designer Bob Gurr would design the boat system (which he would later adapt for Pirates of the Caribbean).

Walt called Mary Blair out of retirement and made her art director of the project. She had accompanied Walt on his 1941 goodwill tour of Latin America and had learned exciting ways to use color. She also had a special ability to see the world through the eyes of a child. Blair created unique color schemes for each continent: blue and green for Africa, hot-yellow for the Middle East, pink-orange for Latin America, and multiple hues for Europe.

Walt assigned his favorite songwriters, Richard Sherman and Robert Sherman, to write the theme song. The Sherman brothers were accustomed to producing many songs, out of which Walt might choose one or two. The first song they wrote for Children of the World came so quickly and easily, the brothers doubted that it could be good enough for the attraction. The tune and the lyrics were catchy, but simple. "It's just a first try," they said before they played it. Walt listened—then he said, "That's perfect!" He loved the song so much, he renamed the attraction. It was no longer Children of the World, but "it's a small world."

The historical time frame in which Walt and his Imagineers worked is significant. The world had just survived the October 1962 Cuban missile crisis, which had brought the US and USSR within an eye-blink of nuclear war. Walt and his creative team wanted to promote the World's Fair theme of "Peace through Understanding." Walt's urgent sense of mission inspired them to accomplish an incredibly difficult Imagineering feat in a mere eleven months.

"It's a small world" opened at the World's Fair as a fifteen-minute-long water-based dark ride featuring more than 300 Audio-Animatronic doll-like children. After the Fair closed, Walt moved the attraction to Disneyland, where it replaced the Fantasyland Railroad Depot. The "it's a small world" façade and show building were located just north of the tracks, so that the train passes immediately in front of the façade. The attraction opened to Disneyland guests on May 28, 1966. Today, every Disney theme park has its own "it's a small world."

Rolly Crump, assisted by Jack Fergus, created toys based on paintings by Mary Blair. Motivated by the deadline crunch, Rolly invented a super-quick way of carving toys and dolls out of Styrofoam, covering them with papier-mâché (made from paper towels dipped in water-thinned glue), then brushing them with glue for a smooth, permanent finish. The toy or doll was lightweight, appeared to be carved from wood, and could be assembled quickly. Rolly and Jack were able to complete one toy or doll per day.

"I'd never done anything like that before," Rolly later recalled, "and I was surprised at how well my unproven method worked."[199] In the years since he created those figures, many have been replaced by more durable fiberglass figures, but some of the dolls and toys in the attraction are originals, hand-built in 1963. Rolly has visited the attraction in recent years and says he can't tell the papier-mâché figures from the fiberglass.

Rolly recalled how a thoughtful gift from Walt impacted the design of "it's a small world." Walt had returned to the studio from Europe with a gift-wrapped box. "Happy birthday, Rolly," Walt said.

It wasn't Rolly's birthday, but he thanked Walt and opened the box. Inside was a toy bicyclist riding on a tightwire between two poles. By raising and lowering either pole, you could make the cyclist go backward or forward. Rolly's first thought was that he could use the same principle to add a tightrope-riding cyclist to "it's a small world." With the help of Yale Gracey, Rolly built a larger and more elaborate version, with two riders and a balance beam, plus an automated mechanism to keep the bicycle moving back and forth across the wire as the boats floated beneath it.

Rolly installed it, then invited Walt to come see it. "Walt," he said, "we took that little birthday gift you gave me and made a bigger one." Then Rolly demonstrated the tightrope cyclist.

Without warning, Walt reached out and tugged on the weight that kept the wire taut, shaking it up and down.

"Walt," Rolly shouted, "what are you doing?"

"I want to make sure the bicycle won't come off the wire and hit someone on the head." Once Walt was satisfied that the bicycle was safe, he okayed it.[200]

Unfortunately, Rolly Crump's bicycle on a tightrope was removed during one of the attraction's refurbishments, probably in 2005. But the story of Walt's kindness to Rolly lives on, reminding us that when a leader serves his people, they will repay that service with ingenuity, creativity, and efforts that are above and beyond the call of duty.

Some people scoff at "it's a small world" because of its sedate pace and the simple, repetitive song that lodges in your brain. We live in a cynical age where Walt's kind of sentiment is often scorned as "corny." Compared to the hyper-speed thrills of the Matterhorn Bobsleds or Space Mountain, some say the gentle, tuneful sweetness of "it's a small world" is only for little children and grandmas. I disagree.

"It's a small world" is a gift of hope from a leader who was a servant to the world. It's a gift of color and song and joy, expressing Walt's desire to bless the children of the world with a message of harmony and peace. It will be a sad day for the human race if the world ever becomes so jaded and cynical that there is no room in a Disney theme park for "it's a small world."

A Servant of His Country

During World War I, sixteen-year-old Walt Disney volunteered for military service but was turned down by both the army and the navy for being too young. He applied to the Red Cross and was accepted as an ambulance driver, but only because he falsified his birthdate on his passport application. From his youth to end of his life, Walt Disney was a willing servant of his country.

He once said, "I get red, white, and blue at times."[201] Walt wore his patriotism on his sleeve. On Disneyland's opening day, he read the inscription from the dedication plaque at the base of the Town Square flagpole: "Disneyland is dedicated to the ideals, the dreams, and the hard facts that have created America."

At the Town Square at around 4:30 every afternoon, Disneyland conducts a Flag Retreat ceremony—a patriotic display initiated by Walt himself on the park's opening day. Whenever Walt was in the park, he would watch the flag-raising and flag-lowering ceremonies from his apartment window over the Fire House.

The ceremony has changed very little since 1955. The Disneyland Band plays and the Dapper Dans sing patriotic standards like "You're a Grand Old Flag" and "America the Beautiful." The band also plays official hymns of each military branch. Disneyland invites veterans and active-duty members of the military to stand at the flagpole and be recognized. As the band plays "The Star-Spangled Banner," the flag is reverently lowered and folded. The ceremony lasts about twenty minutes.

Walt's Disneyland, once jeered as "that kiddie park out in Anaheim" or "Disney's Folly," has hosted some of the great leaders and dignitaries of America and around the world. One of the first dignitaries to visit was the sitting vice president, Richard M. Nixon. He took his family to Disneyland on August 11, 1955, just three weeks after opening day. Nixon told a reporter, "This is a paradise for children and for grown-ups, too." The vice president and his family returned to Disneyland in June 1959 and took part in ribbon-cutting ceremonies for three new Tomorrowland attractions, the Matterhorn Bobsleds, the Disneyland Monorail, and the Submarine Voyage.

Former President Harry S. Truman and his wife Bess visited Disneyland in November 1957, less than five years after he left office. The Disneyland Band played "I'm Just Wild About Harry" and the "Missouri Waltz" as the Trumans toured the park. The former president remarked that Disneyland's Main Street USA reminded him of his hometown, Independence, Missouri. Truman walked so briskly from one attraction to the next that Disneyland guides and photographers struggled to keep up. His favorite attraction was the riverboat *Mark Twain*, which he steered from the pilot house. In Fantasyland, the former leader of the Democratic Party refused to board the Dumbo ride. "Make it a donkey," he said, "and I'll do it."[202]

In November 1959, Massachusetts senator (and presidential primary candidate) John F. Kennedy held an informal meeting with a foreign dignitary on Disneyland's Main Street USA. JFK was a youthful forty-two at the time and needed a photo op with a foreign leader to increase his gravitas. During a campaign swing through California, he arranged to meet Sékou Touré, president of Guinea, West Africa. Kennedy arrived by helicopter at the Disneyland helipad. He met President Touré on the Disneyland Railroad platform, then the two leaders went to City Hall for a half-hour conversation in French and English. Afterwards, Kennedy toured Disneyland, shaking hands and introducing himself to potential voters.

In December 1961, months after leaving office, former President Dwight D. Eisenhower took his wife Mamie, son John, daughter-in-law Barbara, and his four grandchildren to Disneyland. He sat in the driver's seat of Bob Gurr's fire engine and waved a fireman's hat to the crowd on Main Street. In Adventureland, he took the wheel of the *Yangtze Lotus* on the Jungle Cruise. The former president and first lady relaxed in Walt's apartment over the Fire House while the younger members of the Eisenhower clan enjoyed Fantasyland.

In Frontierland, the Eisenhowers rode the *Mark Twain* and enjoyed the Wild West show at the Golden Horseshoe Saloon. Disneyland's resident comedian Wally Boag gave Ike's six-year-old granddaughter Mary Jean a balloon and said, "Give it to your granddad. If he learns to blow it up, he'll be a big man in his neighborhood." Eisenhower laughed uproariously. At the end of the day, Ike said he had more fun at Disneyland than his grandchildren did.[203]

A scheduling conflict prevented Walt from meeting the former president in Disneyland that day, but a little more than a year later, on February 22, 1963, Ike presented Walt with the George Washington Medal of Honor at a gala dinner in Palm Springs. The medal, awarded by the Freedoms Foundation at Valley Forge, honors people who display exceptional patriotism and good citizenship. Eisenhower (who founded the organization in 1949) called Walt the "Ambassador of

Freedom for the United States of America" for his "patriotic dedication in advancing the concept of freedom under God; for his unfailing professional devotion to the things which matter most, human dignity and personal responsibility; for masterful creative leadership in communicating the hopes and aspirations of our free society to the far corners of the planet."

In response, Walt humbly replied, "I think I should make a little confession. And that is that personally, I don't understand why the heck it was given to me. I've just been going along doing what sort of comes naturally to me.... If you could see close in my eyes, the American flag is waving in both of them, and up my spine is growing this red, white and blue stripe. I'm very proud and very honored. Thank you."[204]

Walt's last known visit to Disneyland took place on October 14, 1966. That day, he hosted a personal salute to all the living recipients of the Medal of Honor and their families. The heroes rode down Main Street aboard Disneyland's fleet of vehicles—the Omnibus, the Horseless Carriage, the horse-drawn Trolley, and the Fire Engine. At the Main Street Opera House, Walt took the stage and introduced a special performance of Great Moments with Mr. Lincoln.

In his welcoming remarks, Walt told his guests he was personally at their service. "Around Disneyland," he said, "I'm the top kick. I run the show here. And I'm telling you that if they don't treat you right—you report it to me.... We've got a nice menu laid out for you and it's going to be a busy day.... It's a real privilege and an honor to welcome you folks here today."[205]

Walt rolled out the red carpet for these highly decorated American heroes. It was a typical act of service by a great leader with a serving heart. Walt loved to use his motion pictures, his cartoon characters, and his theme park to project American values of freedom and fair play around the world. He loved to use his creations to honor and bless the lives of deserving people like the Medal of Honor recipients and their families.

On November 2, about two weeks after the Medal of Honor event at Disneyland, Walt entered St. Joseph's Hospital, across the street from the Disney Studio. He had been suffering from neck pain for weeks. X-rays showed an ominous spot on Walt's left lung that later proved to be cancer. He died on December 15, 1966, after a life of extraordinary service to his nation and to American ideals.

A Servant to Children

In a July 1953 column in the *Los Angeles Times*, Hedda Hopper wrote, "Each Christmas my granddaughter Joan receives an exquisite selection of toys from a fellow named Walt Disney. The gifts, though making her squeal with delight, always puzzled her. Until recently she had never seen a regular movie and her first was *Peter Pan*, so to her Walt was as mysterious and remote as Santa Claus. Even when he gave a birthday party for Joan and her friends, Walt was not to be seen, so Joan became suspicious. 'Is there really a Walt Disney?' she asked me."[206]

Well, yes, Joan, there really was a Walt Disney, and he was a servant to children. One of the least-reported dimensions of Walt's multifaceted personality is the depth of his compassion for children. Despite his busy schedule, he continually made time for acts of personal kindness and caring. And unlike many corporate leaders who make a big show of their "charity," Walt wanted no publicity. His compassion and acts of service to children came straight from his serving heart.

In June 1955, as Disneyland's opening day grew closer and construction of the park was far from complete, a letter arrived at the Burbank studio from a mother in the eastern United States. Her seven-year-old son was dying of leukemia and had two last wishes. One was to meet kiddie-show host Pinky Lee (a baggy-pants, slapstick comic with the catchphrase "Oooh! You make me so *mad*!"). His second wish: to ride Walt's Santa Fe and Disneyland Railroad, which he had seen under construction on the *Disneyland* TV show. The family had already set out for California when the letter arrived at the studio.

When the family reached Los Angeles, the mother called the studio, and Walt's secretary told her to be at Disneyland on Saturday morning. Walt met the family in the parking lot. He bent down to the boy and said, "I understand you want to see my train. Well, let's go!" He scooped the boy up in his arms and carried him to the train station. Together, Walt and the boy watched cranes lifting railroad cars from flatbed trucks and lowering them onto the rails. Once the locomotive and cars were coupled together, the engineer fired up the boiler. Then Walt took the boy into the cab for the train's maiden journey around the park. The train pulled out of the station, and Walt pointed out all the attractions to the boy.

After the train ride, Walt went to his car, then returned with a package—a gold-framed piece of original animation art from his just-released animated feature, *Lady and the Tramp*. Walt placed the package in the boy's hands, then told his parents, "Well, we really saw the place. He liked my train."

When the family had left, Walt instructed his staff: "No publicity!" Many of Walt's employees witnessed Walt's act of compassion for a dying little boy, and they kept his secret during his lifetime. A few years after Walt's death, Bob Jani—Walt's first director of special events (and the originator of Disneyland's Main Street Electrical Parade)—told the story to Walt's biographer Bob Thomas.[207]

In early November 1966, Walt and Lillian, accompanied by family and associates, arrived in Williamsburg, Virginia, for the American Forestry Association's annual conference. There Walt was to be honored with the AFA's Distinguished Service Award for his nature films and support for the environment. The event would also feature a Walt Disney Film Festival, including *Bambi*, a Donald Duck / Chip 'n Dale cartoon *Winter Storage*, the live-action comedy *Yellowstone Cubs*, and a documentary about smoke jumpers, *A Fire Called Jeremiah*.

Walt was in a lot of pain due to his yet-to-be diagnosed cancer. During their stay, Walt and his party dined at Williamsburg's famed King's Arms Tavern. As they were seated around a large table, a young waiter, dressed in a Revolutionary War–era costume, introduced himself to Walt as Ken Lounsbery. Walt recognized him instantly as the son of animator John Lounsbery, one of "Disney's Nine Old Men." As a boy, Ken had visited many times at Walt's Carolwood Drive home and had ridden Walt's backyard railroad. He had also worked summers at the Burbank studio. Walt turned to his wife and said, "Why, it's Kenny. Lillian, look here, it's Johnny's son!"

Ken Lounsbery was working at the King's Arms while attending the College of William and Mary. He would always remember the night Walt was so happy to see him.[208]

During those last few months of Walt's life, one of his secretaries, Lucille Martin, became alarmed about Walt's health. Years later, she told me in a phone interview, "Walt was unwell much of the time. He was sometimes discouraged about his health, and he was concerned about what would happen to the company's stock value if anything happened to him. He worried about the future of his projects, EPCOT and CalArts. And he was also very concerned about the people around him. He was one of the kindest men I have ever known.

"When I started working for him in 1965, I was alone with two young children. He was always asking about my girls and how we were doing. One day, Walt was sitting in his office with another secretary, Tommie Wilck, and me. It was near the end of the day and he was very tired. As he stood up to leave for the day, he said, 'Sometimes I feel like chucking it all.' Then he smiled and added, 'But Lucille and her girls need me.' I've always treasured that. He went into the hospital just a few days later."

Walt cared deeply about young people, their dreams, and their future. He communicated hope and encouragement to the next generation. He once said, "To the youngsters of today, I say believe in the future, the world is getting better; there still is plenty of opportunity. Why, would you believe it, when I was a kid I thought it was already too late for me to make good at anything."[209]

Walt Disney made good in large part because he was a leader who served, and a servant who led.

Walt's Utopian Dream

In May 2019, I had Disney expert Christopher Lyons on my radio show. Chris is the author of *Top Disney*, a book of Disney lists published in 2019. I asked him, "Would you consider Walt one of the five most influential people of the past hundred years?"

"Absolutely," Chris said. "In fact, I'd put him at number one. He has influenced not just millions of people but billions of people around the world. That influence will never diminish. It will only keep expanding."

Now, that's a strong statement, especially when you consider all the presidents, prime ministers, kings, dictators, and other influential figures of the past century. But I am inclined to agree. Walt might just be number one on that list. Most leaders come to power, win a couple of elections, deal with this war or that economic crisis, and then fade into history. Walt's influence goes on and on.

Dick Nunis began his Disneyland career in 1955 as an attraction operator. He rose to become chairman of Walt Disney Attractions and a key executive in the development of Walt Disney World and other Disney theme parks. Nunis remembers Walt as a leader with a utopian dream of the future. He recalled a day in 1962 when Walt gave evangelist Billy Graham a tour of Disneyland. Walt and Billy had just stepped off a riverboat on the Jungle Cruise. Standing on the dock, Graham turned to Walt and said, "What a fantastic world! What a marvelous world of fantasy!"

"Billy," Walt replied, "look around you. Look at all the people. All nationalities. All languages. All smiling. All having fun together. Billy, this is the real world. The fantasy is outside."

Nunis concluded, "I never forgot that. And I think that's what we're all about."[210]

That's certainly what Walt was all about. He was not merely putting on a show and counting up his profits. He was offering the world his vision of a possible future—a utopian future. He wanted the world to see his visionary "real world" of peace, joy, and wonder. To him, the world of international tensions, racial conflict, and petty hatreds was a dark and disturbed fantasy that need not exist. He envisioned a better world—a world beyond hatred and division—and he showcased that vision in his movies and in his magical kingdom, Disneyland.

When I interviewed Art Linkletter in 2004, he told me about

his involvement, alongside Walt, in the 1960 Winter Olympics in Squaw Valley, California. Some critics derisively dubbed it the "Disney Olympics," but athletes, officials, and spectators praised it as the best-produced Olympic event in history. Walt brought some of Hollywood's biggest names to the Olympic Village to welcome and entertain the competitors—Jack Benny, Bing Crosby, Danny Kaye, Jayne Mansfield, Roy Rogers, Red Skelton, and more.

The night before the opening ceremonies, a blizzard blanketed the roads and CBS sportscaster Chris Schenkel couldn't reach his broadcast location. No problem. Walt Disney and Art Linkletter went on the air in his place, providing commentary as the Olympic torch completed its 9,000-mile journey, the bands played the Olympic theme, and 2,000 white doves were released to the sky.

Over the days that followed, Walt oversaw the shows for the athletes and Art emceed them. "It was an amazing experience," Art told me. "At every table, there was a different language spoken. One night, Walt looked around at all the tables, with athletes from around the world, representing every race and language. His eyes were shining, and he said to me, 'Isn't this an amazing sight? Look at these people! They've come from all over the world, and they're all here, sharing the same hopes and dreams. This is how the whole world should be.' He was very moved by that. It was like a dream come true."

At the 1960 Olympics and in Disneyland, Walt saw the realization of his utopian dream of a world at peace. He saw people of all nations and races and faiths coming together in harmony. He believed it could happen anywhere, given the right environment. Walt dedicated himself to creating that kind of environment, not only in his motion pictures but also in such projects as California Institute of the Arts (CalArts), the 1960 Winter Olympics, the 1964 New York World's Fair, his vision for the Experimental Prototype Community of Tomorrow (EPCOT), and, of course, Disneyland.

When Walt opened Disneyland to the public on July 18, 1955, people came not only from around California but from around the world. According to a Disneyland press release from July 18, 1956, nearly four million visitors passed through the turnstiles during the park's first year, making Disneyland "the largest single private enterprise attraction in the Western Hemisphere." An estimated 41 percent of Disneyland's guests came from out-of-state, and many of those came from sixty-four nations "including such far-off places as Saudi Arabia, Iceland, Liechtenstein and even the Soviet Union."[211]

Many of Walt's guests in those early years were foreign heads of state. President Achmed Sukarno of Indonesia visited Disneyland with his twelve-year-old son Guntur in June 1956. Walt served as their personal tour guide to the Magic Kingdom. Prime Minister Huseyn Shaheed Suhrawardy of Pakistan visited Disneyland in July 1957. The Shah of Iran and Empress Farah visited the park in April 1962.

In November 1961, Prime Minister Jawaharlal Nehru of India visited the United States for ten days, conferring with President Kennedy and addressing the UN General Assembly before heading to Disneyland. Walt served as the tour guide and chauffeur of India's head of state, driving Nehru and his forty-four-year-old daughter Indira down Main Street in one of Disneyland's two "jitneys" (fringe-topped horseless carriages). Indira would herself become Prime Minister of India a little more than four years later. Speaking to reporters, she said, "We looked forward to Disneyland as much as anything on our trip."[212]

One of the most fascinating stories of a foreign dignitary at Disneyland involved King Mohammed V of Morocco, who visited the park in December 1957. The king is remembered for protecting the Moroccan

Jewish community from the Vichy government's anti-Jewish laws during World War II. After Nazi Germany ordered the Vichy government to round up and deport Morocco's 250,000 Jews to Nazi concentration camps, King Mohammed courageously defied the order.

King Mohammed arrived at Disneyland in the morning, and Walt was on hand to give him a personally guided four-hour tour of the Magic Kingdom. The king's morning visit was accompanied by ceremonies, photographers, reporters, and security guards. King Mohammed was so captivated by Disneyland that he and his aides returned to their hotel suite, changed into American-style clothing, and returned to the park for a second visit—this time, in disguise.

The king and his aides paid their admission and passed through the turnstiles like any other guests. They stood in line and enjoyed the rides throughout the afternoon. At one point, a Disneyland executive recognized King Mohammed and approached him, offering to again roll out the official red carpet. The Moroccan king said he wanted no guides, no photographers, and no publicity. He wanted to enjoy Disneyland as a normal paying customer—and he did.

Walt was one of America's greatest and most influential ambassadors to the world. He built Disneyland, and great leaders and ordinary people came from around the globe to see his magical kingdom. Disneyland is a monument to American ingenuity, American freedom, and the American spirit of enterprise and achievement.

When Walt's friend Ray Bradbury urged him to run for mayor of Los Angeles, Walt smiled and wisely replied, "Oh, Ray, why should I be mayor when I'm already king?"[213]

During the eleven years that Walt ruled his Magic Kingdom in Anaheim, kings, prime ministers, and presidents passed through Disneyland's gates. Many of those world leaders caught a glimpse of

Walt's utopian dream for humanity. The world has moved farther from the fulfillment of that dream ever since Walt passed away.

But perhaps if you and I and thousands of others would learn to lead and serve like Walt, who knows...?

How to Lead Like Walt

In mid-1951, Hedda Hopper went to the Disney studio in Burbank for a preview screening of *Alice in Wonderland*. Walt wasn't present, but one of his top executives was on hand to answer her questions. When the movie ended, the Disney exec said, "I want to show you Walt's latest project."

He guided Hopper to the studio machine shop. There, to the surprise of both of them, they found Walt. He was at a work bench, all alone, tinkering with his one-eighth scale live steam locomotive, the *Lilly Belle* ("live steam" means steam under pressure). Walt and Hedda were old friends, and he greeted her warmly. He didn't ask her what she thought of *Alice in Wonderland*. Instead, he pointed to the *Lilly Belle* and said, "Hedda, every time I begin to think myself a big shot, I come to this shop, work with my hands, and learn humility."[214]

Walt was a great leader because he had a strong ego, a confident sense of his place in the world, combined with a deep sense of authentic humility. Even though he had long since given up cartooning, he still liked to work with his hands. Tinkering with his backyard railroad helped him maintain his perspective and his common touch.

His love of live steam railroading reflected Walt's childlike side. He had loved trains ever since he was a boy. It was a childhood obsession that he never outgrew. In his manhood, he never forgot the joys and fascinations of his boyhood. He continued to be intrigued by magic and fantasy, knights and fair maidens, castles and kingdoms, Tom Sawyer and Mississippi riverboats, pioneers and pirates, Abraham Lincoln and Davy Crockett, rocket ships and submarines. Above all, he maintained his love for coal-fired steam-powered trains.

Walt's railroading obsession met with strong opposition at home. His wife Lillian hated Walt's Carolwood Pacific Railroad (named for the street he lived on). Just as she had opposed *Snow White* and Disneyland, she tried to talk Walt out of his live steam obsession. In the October 1965 issue of *Railroad Magazine*, he wrote:

> [Lillian] didn't take kindly to the idea of having a railroad run around our house, and told me so in no uncertain terms. Things came to such an impasse that I went to my lawyer and had him draw up a right-of-way agreement giving me permission to operate the railroad on the property. My wife signed it and my daughters witnessed the agreement.
>
> I figured out a route around the place, but it required a six-foot cut in one of the slopes. This time my wife put her foot down. So I compromised by building a tunnel ninety feet long and covering it with dirt. I gave my secretary strict instructions not to tell me how much it cost.[215]

Walt spent many happy hours building the Carolwood Pacific and giving guests of all ages rides on his model railroad. He would sit on the tender (the car behind the locomotive that stored water and coal to fuel the train) and his guests would ride on the boxcars and flatcars.

One time, he was in the backyard alone, experimenting with a cable control that allowed him to sit on the first passenger car instead of the tender. The cable enabled him to remotely operate the throttle and brakes. He started up the train to test the new control. As the train rounded a turn, the locomotive's front wheel struck a rock on the track. The engine wobbled and uncoupled from the tender. The jolt knocked Walt backwards, causing him to yank the control cable which pulled the throttle valve wide open. The locomotive accelerated to full speed, a plume of steam shooting high into the air. Walt watched helplessly as the engine raced away from him, out of control and headed for the tunnel.

He jumped off the slowing car and ran through the garden, hoping to catch the runaway engine before it hit the tight curve beyond the tunnel. Just as he reached the end of the tunnel, the locomotive shot out, moving way too fast to catch. It sped into the curve and derailed at top speed. Walt watched helplessly as the engine barrel-rolled down the embankment, cracked off the smoke stack and cow catcher, and came to a stop amid clouds of hissing steam.

Walt surveyed the destruction, then shouted to Lillian, who was in the house, "Come on out if you want to see a terrible sight!"

Lillian came out and saw the broken train engine and her broken-hearted husband. "Oh, Walt," she said, "that's too bad!" And Walt knew she meant it sincerely. Though she had hated that train, she knew Walt loved it, so it saddened her to see it in ruins.

Walt later reflected, "I had finally succeeded in getting her on my side in the railroad operation—but I had to wreck a train to do it."[216]

I think one of the most underappreciated aspects of Walt's personality and his leadership style was his Peter Pan–like refusal to set aside his boyhood obsessions and childlike sense of wonder. Though he was one of the most committed, focused, hard-working, imaginative, and downright *mature* human beings to ever build an organization, he never lost the ability to see the world through the eyes of a child.

Hedda Hopper observed this quality in Walt one time when she visited the Burbank studio. Ventriloquist Edgar Bergen was shooting a scene with his wooden puppet Charlie McCarthy. Hopper recalled, "On a box in an old sweater a man sat hunched forward completely absorbed in the scene. That was Walt. When the camera stopped, Disney shook his head wonderingly. 'That dummy simply kills me,' he said. 'He's amazing.'" Hopper added that one of Walt's studio associates told her, "Everything is a wonder to Walt."[217]

To lead like Walt, we need to hold on to our childhood joys and our childlike wonder. We need to combine the maturity of complete seven-sided leadership with the timeless fascination and wonder of a child.

Walt's "Reverse Pyramid"

Reflecting on Walt's uncommon approach to leadership, Disney historian Jim Korkis noted that there are two basic kinds of leaders—the "servant leader" and the "warrior leader." He says that typical roles for warrior leaders are coaches and military commanders. (I would add that some warrior leaders are also servant leaders. Military commanders like General Matthew Ridgeway, who parachuted into Normandy with his troops on D-Day, was a servant leader. And so were coaches John Wooden of UCLA and Tony Dungy of the Buccaneers and Colts.)

Walt, Korkis said, was a servant leader, the kind of leader who exercises authority but who also "supports the staff, admits mistakes, and actively solicits new perspectives." Walt had his own term for this kind of leadership: the "reverse pyramid." In Walt's reverse pyramid model, leaders are at the bottom instead of the top of the pyramid, and every decision they make, every word they speak, every action they take is intended to support everyone else in the organization, from the janitors and secretaries to the top executives.

Having made a careful study of how Walt led his company, I agree with Jim Korkis that Walt was a true servant leader. Not a perfect leader, but definitely a leader who served from the bottom of the reverse pyramid. Korkis summarized Walt's strengths as a leader this way:

> Disney was a charismatic, passionate, visionary leader who inspired his followers to consistently exceed what they thought was possible and to explore unfamiliar disciplines. He established both formal and informal channels of communication, often directly approaching front line workers like gardeners and ticket-takers to get their opinions not only of challenges but possible solutions.... While he was a calculated risk taker, he also took full responsibility for any failure.... Disney believed in his dreams so intensely that it evoked a similar commitment from his staff.

Korkis also listed Walt's weaknesses as a leader—traits that you and I would do well to avoid. Walt had a mercurial temper. When he was in a foul mood, members of his staff would warn each other, "Walt's wearing the bear suit today." Though Walt trusted his staff, he insisted on personally approving every phase of production. As a result, people often had to wait idly for Walt to come around and okay each step of their work—a waste of time, talent, and money.

So Walt was not without his flaws. Yet his virtues far outweighed his flaws, and that's why his achievements are so great and so many. That's why people loved him, remained loyal to him, and helped him achieve his dreams.

Walt once said, "A person should set his goals as early as he can and devote all his energy and talent to getting there. With enough effort, he may achieve it. Or he may find something that is even more rewarding. But in the end, no matter what the outcome, he will know he has been alive."[218] Walt lived and led by that advice. Throughout his career, he truly knew he was alive.

When Walt was no older than fifteen, he dreamed of building an amusement park like Electric Park, "but mine's going to be clean."[219] So he pursued his dream and continually refined his mental vision of it. Finally, when he was in his fifties, he began building it.

There were times when he nearly despaired of ever seeing that dream fulfilled. Even his wife and brother opposed him. The experts ridiculed him. For years, the money he needed to build Disneyland seemed completely out of reach. Even after construction was well underway, there were times when it seemed that the reality would never match the shining vision in his imagination.

Just a few months before the park was scheduled to open, Walt sat glumly on a curb in Disneyland. Next to him sat Harper Goff, who had designed the architecture of Main Street. With tears in his eyes, Walt told Goff that half the construction budget was already spent and "there isn't one thing you'd call terrific out there right now."[220]

Despite his moments of doubt, Walt's Disneyland dream came true—not because he wished upon a star, but because he demonstrated the vision, communication skills, people skills, character, competence, boldness, and the serving heart of a complete seven-sided leader. He dreamed big dreams—impossible dreams, they told him—then he moved heaven and earth to make his dreams come true.

When you, as a leader, start with a vision, then communicate that vision to the people you lead, utilize your people skills to motivate and inspire them, maintain your character and integrity at every decision point, command with competence, lead with boldness and confidence, and support your people with your serving heart—*your vision will become your reality*. And the moment your dream is fulfilled will be a moment of sublime joy and celebration.

Walt experienced that moment on July 17, 1955, the day the gates of Disneyland opened for the very first time. Disneyland had been his dream ever since he was a boy. Now it was a reality. He stood at the window of his apartment over the Fire Station, watching as moms and dads and boys and girls streamed through the gates of his Magic Kingdom and fanned out to discover its rivers and towns, its jungles and deserts, its Castle and Carrousel, its rocket ship and whirling teacups.

At Walt's side in his Fire House apartment were the Mouseketeers, whose TV show, *The Mickey Mouse Club*, would soon premiere on ABC. Mouseketeer Sharon Baird was twelve years old at the time. She later recalled, "I was standing next to him at the window, watching the guests come pouring through the gates. When I looked up at him, he had his hands behind his back, a grin from ear to ear. I could see a lump in his throat and a tear streaming down his cheek. He had realized his dream."[221]

Dreams and Visions

After Disneyland opened, Walt continued to dream big dreams. Mike Vance, who worked at Walt Disney Productions and at Disneyland, recalled an incident in 1966, as Walt was preparing to take on the greatest challenge of his career, the vast complex of theme parks we now know as Walt Disney World in Florida.

Vance noted that Walt had a way of looking at the world around him and observing details that escaped the notice of most people. One morning, Vance arrived at the Burbank studio as a gentle rain was falling. Stepping out of his car, he saw Walt pulling into the studio lot in his Mercedes coupe

Moments later Walt joined Vance, and they strolled through the drizzling rain toward the Animation Building. Along the way, Walt paused for a closer look at a flowering oleander along the sidewalk.

"Look at the tiny water bubble sitting on this leaf," Walt said. "I wonder how that bubble appears to the leaf. It probably looks like a giant dome. You know, we should have a bubble restaurant floating around on a huge leaf on Bay Lake in Florida."

They walked on and Walt added, "Creativity is everywhere. You can't get away from it." As they went, Walt recalled his Missouri boyhood and rainy days and jumping in puddles and the fragrance of wood burning in the fireplace. "Did you ever dream about what you were going to do when you got big?" he added. "Did you ever get the urge to grow up and do everything fast?"

When they reached the steps of the Animation Building, Walt paused and said, "Do you want to know something more exciting than what we've been talking about? It's to be an adult like we are now and look back through the window of memory, remembering the time when we were little children, but it's even more exciting to know that we became the kind of people we dreamed about as children. Do you know what that's called? Fulfillment! . . . I hope you have that kind of feeling in your life, Mike. I hope you become what you dreamed you could be when you were a little boy."

Mike Vance concluded, "This was Walt at his purest and best. This was the Walt the world came to love and admire. He wasn't a false image. He was real."[222]

Walt didn't live to build his last, greatest, most challenging vision. He had an appointment with eternity. On December 15, 1966, he kept it.

On the night before he died, as he lay in a hospital bed across the street from the studio that Snow White built, Walt mapped out his vision for the Florida project on the ceiling tiles overhead. He was a visionary leader to the very end.

Walt's brother Roy oversaw the construction of the Florida resort, which was to be called Disney World. Shortly before the resort opened to the public on October 1, 1971, Roy announced that the official title would be Walt Disney World. He wanted the world to remember that the Florida resort was the fulfillment of Walt's dream.

Many people who had known Walt were on hand the day Walt Disney World was dedicated, including Mike Vance. After the opening ceremony, someone commented to him, "Isn't it too bad Walt Disney didn't live to see this?"

Vance replied, "He did see it. That's why it's here."[223]

Walt's vision was so clear, and the force of his leadership was so strong, that even death couldn't stop his vision from going forward. That's the legacy of a bold, serving, visionary leader. Your dreams and visions can live long after you....

When you lead like Walt.

Acknowledgments

J **DEEPLY APPRECIATE THE SUPPORT** and guidance of the people who helped make this book possible:

Special thanks to Alex Martins, Dan DeVos, and Joel Glass of the Orlando Magic.

Hats off to my associate Andrew Herdliska; my proofreader, Ken Hussar; and my ace typist, Fran Thomas.

Thanks also to my writing partner, Jim Denney, for his superb contributions in shaping this manuscript.

Hearty thanks also go to Peter Vegso, Allison Janse, and the entire HCI team for their vision and insight, and for believing we had something important to say in these pages.

A special thanks to Peggy Matthews Rose, whose love for Walt and knowledge of his life has immeasurably enriched these pages. I'm grateful also to Brook Lopez and Robin Lopez for their generous foreword, and to Swen Nater for permission to use his poem in these pages.

And, finally, special thanks and appreciation go to my wife, Ruth, and to my wonderful and supportive family. They are truly the backbone of my life.

About the Authors

Pat Williams was senior vice president of the Orlando Magic, an NBA team he cofounded in 1987. Pat has been involved in professional sports for more than fifty-seven years and has been affiliated with NBA teams in Chicago, Atlanta, and Philadelphia, including the 1983 World Champion Philadelphia 76ers. He is one of America's top motivational and inspirational speakers and the author of 111 books, including *Go for the Magic, How to Be Like Mike, How to Be Like Jesus, How to Be Like Walt, The Paradox of Power, 21 Great Leaders, Leadership Excellence, Leading God's Way, The Success Intersection: What Happens When Your Talent Meets Your Passion, Coach Wooden: The 7 Principles That Shaped His Life and Will Change Yours,* and *Coach Wooden's Forgotten Teams.* He has written on subjects ranging from sports to humor to marriage and family to success and motivation. He hosts three weekly talk radio shows in Orlando—a sports show, a Christian show, and a general news talk show.

In great demand as a motivational, inspirational, and humorous speaker, Pat Williams has addressed employees from most of the Fortune 500 companies, in addition to being a featured speaker at two Billy Graham crusades. He has run fifty-eight marathons, climbed Mount Rainier, and is a weight lifter and a serious baseball fan (before his long career in the NBA, he spent seven years with the Philadelphia Phillies organization, two as a player and five in the front office, plus three years in the front office of the Minnesota Twins organization). Pat and his wife Ruth live in Winter Park, Florida.

Jim Denney is a professional writer with more than 130 books to his credit, including *Walt's Disneyland, Writing in Overdrive,* and the Timebenders science-fantasy series for young readers (beginning with *Battle Before Time*). He lives in southern California and is a member of Science Fiction and Fantasy Writers of America (SFWA).

CONTACT

If you'd like to speak with Pat personally, call (407) 721-0922

Visit Pat Williams's Web site at:
www.PatWilliams.com

If you would like to set up a speaking engagement for Pat, please call contact The Pat Williams Group at: speaking@PatWilliams.com. We would love to hear from you. Please send your comments about this book to Pat Williams at the above address. Thank you.

NOTES

1 Gene Handsaker, "Turning 65, Walt Disney Sees 'No Magic' For Success," Frederick (Maryland) *News*, November 28, 1966, 12.

2 Floyd Norman, "Why My Boss, Walt Disney, Was The Ultimate Business Leader," *Fast Company*, December 15, 2016, https://www.fastcompany.com/3066382/why-my-boss-walt-disney-was-the-ultimate-business-leader.

3 Walt Disney, "The Marceline I Knew," letter to *The Marceline News*, published September 2, 1938, posted by Werner Weiss, Yesterland.com, April 16, 2010, https://www.yesterland.com/marceline.html.

4 Brian Burnes, Dan Viets, and Robert W. Butler, *Walt Disney's Missouri: The Roots of a Creative Genius* (Kansas City, Missouri: Kansas City Star Books, 2002), 61.

5 Howard Hendricks, *Color Outside the Lines* (Nashville: Thomas Nelson, 1998), xiii.

6 John Bordsen, "This Tiny Town is the Site of Disney's 'Lost' Park," CNN, June 12, 2018, https://www.cnn.com/travel/article/marceline-missouri-lost-disney-park/index.html.

7 Robin Seaton Jefferson, "Inside Walt Disney's Life in Marceline," MissouriLife.com, October 23, 2017, https://www.missourilife.com/inside-walt-disneys-life-in-marceline/.

8 Charles Champlin, "Disney's Legacy as a Showman," *Los Angeles Times*, December 19, 1966, Part 5, 30.

9 Jefferson, "Inside Walt Disney's Life in Marceline."

10 Katherine Greene and Richard Greene, *The Man Behind the Magic: The Story of Walt Disney* (New York: Viking, 1998), 138.

11 Walt Disney, "Give Me the Movies," (Danville) *Kentucky Advocate*, September 1, 1938, 3.

12 Staff writer, "Chicago Federal Building Bombed," (Portland) Morning Oregonian, September 5, 1918, 1; Jeff Dixon, "We Almost Never Heard of Walt Disney," KeysToTheKingdomBook.com, September 4, 2013, http://www.keytothekingdombook.com/wordpress/2013/09/we-almost-never-heard-of-walt-disney/; Tony Tallarico, "It Happened Today: September 4," ThisDayInDisneyHistory.com, http://www.thisdayindisneyhistory.com/Sep04.html.

13 Author uncredited, "Mickey Mouse Creator Young: Disney a Success before Most Men Get Start in Career," Hamilton (Ohio) *Daily News*, March 3, 1932, 9.

14 Jim Korkis, *Walt's Words: Quotations of Walt Disney with Sources* (Orlando: Theme Park Press, 2016), 119.

15 Kathy Merlock Jackson, ed., *Walt Disney: Conversations* (Jackson: University Press of Mississippi, 2006), 62–63.

16 E. B. Radcliffe, "Ready to Quit Twice, Disney Notes, Tracing 20 Years of Movie Production," *Cincinnati Enquirer*, January 23, 1949, 78.

17 Classified ad, "Young Lady for Ink Tracing Work," *Los Angeles Times*, May 24, 1925, Part 4, 3.

18 Bob Thomas, *Building a Company: Roy O. Disney and the Creation of an Entertainment Empire* (New York: Hyperion, 1998), 53.

19 Bob Thomas, *Walt Disney: An American Original* (New York: Disney Editions, 1994), 114–15.

20 Charles Champlin, "Disney's Legacy as a Showman," 30.

21 Wade Sampson, "Saludos Walt," MousePlanet.com, September 23, 2009, https://www.mouseplanet.com/8985/Saludos_Walt.

22 Keith Gluck, "Walt and the Goodwill Tour," Walt Disney Family Museum, September 8, 2016, https://www.waltdisney.org/blog/walt-and-goodwill-tour.

23 Neal Gabler, *Walt Disney: The Triumph of the American Imagination* (New York: Vintage, 2007), 400.

24 Jim Korkis, "Walt Disney's Leadership," MousePlanet.com, December 4, 2013, https://www.mouseplanet.com/10543/Walt_Disneys_Leadership.

25 John Geirland, "Bradbury's Tomorrowland," *Wired*, October 1, 1998, https://www.wired.com/1998/10/bradbury/.

26 Randy Bright, *Disneyland: Inside Story* (New York: Harry N. Abrams, 1987), 33.

27 Jim Denney, "Walt's Disneyland Dream—Was it Older Than Mickey Mouse?," MouseInfo.com, August 28, 2017, https://www.mouseinfo.com/new/2017/08/walts-disneyland-dream-was-it-older-than-mickey-mouse/.

28 Keith Gluck, "Walt's Main Street—Part One: Inspirations," The Disney Project, February 5, 2013, http://disneyproject.com/2013/02/walts-main-street-part-one-inspirations.html.

29 Todd James Pierce, *Three Years in Wonderland: The Disney Brothers, C. V. Wood, and the Making of the Great American Theme Park* (Jackson, MS: University Press of Mississippi, 2016), 41.

30 Gabler, *Walt Disney*, 502.

31 Marylin Hudson, "Diversions: Readings from the Bookshelf," *Orange Coast Magazine*, April 2007, 64.

32 Pat Williams, *How to Be Like Walt: Capturing the Disney Magic Every Day of Your Life* (Deerfield Beach, FL: Health Communications, Inc., 2004), 190.

33 Bob Thomas, *Building a Company: Roy O. Disney and the Creation of an Entertainment Empire* (New York: Hyperion, 1998), 183. Correction: Thomas incorrectly stated that the 1950 and 1951 Disney Christmas specials both aired on NBC. As I've noted, the 1951 special aired on CBS.

34 Some versions of this story state that it was Walt's top aide Dick Irvine who placed the call to Ryman, then Walt took over the call. When Ryman recalled these events, he did not mention Dick Irvine.

35 Don Peri, *Working with Walt: Interviews with Disney Artists* (Jackson, Mississippi: University Press of Mississippi, 2008), 175–177.

36 Thomas, *Building a Company*, 184.

37 Williams, *How to Be Like Walt*, 193.

38 Aline Mosby, "Walt Disney Making Gaudy Debut on Television," Columbus (Indiana) *Republic*, May 15, 1954, 13.

39 Marty Sklar (interview), "Dream it! Do It!," OhMyDisney.com, September 4, 2013, https://ohmy.disney.com/insider/2013/09/04/dream-it-do-it/.

40 Williams, *How to Be Like Walt*, 294.

41 David Meerman Scott and Richard Jurek, *Marketing the Moon: The Selling of the Apollo Lunar Program* (Cambridge, MA: MIT Press, 2014), 15.

42 Billy Watkins, *Apollo Moon Missions: The Unsung Heroes* (Lincoln, NB: University of Nebraska Press, 2005), 5.

43 Billy Watkins, *Apollo Moon Missions*, 8–12.

44 Bill Capodagli and Lynn Jackson, *The Disney Way: Harnessing the Management Secrets of Disney in Your Company* (New York: McGraw-Hill, 2002), 1.

45 Williams, *How to Be Like Walt*, 83.

46 Disney Book Group, *Walt Disney Imagineering: A Behind the Dreams Look at Making the Magic Real* (New York: Disney Editions, 1996), 14.

47 Michael Barrier, "Interviews: Ward Kimball," MichaelBarrier.com, August 2003, http://www.michaelbarrier.com/Interviews/Kimball/interview_ward_kimball.htm.

48 Bob Thomas, "Disneyland a Big Success," Mt. Vernon (Illinois) *Register News*, January 15, 1958, 9.

49 Greg Van Gompel, *Excelsior Amusement Park: Playland of the Twin Cities* (Charleston, SC: The History Press, 2017), 87–89.

50 Gabler, *Walt Disney*, 525.

51 Steven Watts, *The Magic Kingdom: Walt Disney and the American Way of Life* (Columbia,: University of Missouri Press, 1997), 402.

52 Watts, *The Magic Kingdom,* 402.

53 Brian Burnes, Dan Viets, and Robert W. Butler, *Walt Disney's Missouri: The Roots of a Creative Genius* (Kansas City, MO: Kansas City Star Books, 2002), 28.

54 Jefferson, "Inside Walt Disney's Life in Marceline."

55 J. B. Kaufman, *The Fairest One of All: The Making of Walt Disney's Snow White and the Seven Dwarfs* (San Francisco: Walt Disney Family Foundation Press, 2012), 31.

56 Gabler, *Walt Disney*, 217.

57 J. B. Kaufman, *The Fairest One of All*, 31.

58 Gabler, *Walt Disney*, 218.

59 Bob Thomas, *The Walt Disney Biography* (New York: Simon & Schuster, 1977), 24.

60 John G. West, *Walt Disney and Live Action: The Disney Studio's Live-Action Features of the 1950s and 60s* (Orlando: Theme Park Press, 2016), 30–31.

61 Williams, *How to Be Like Walt*, 43.

62 Frank Thomas and Ollie Johnston, *The Illusion of Life: Disney Animation* (New York: Hyperion, 1995), 71.

63 Thomas and Johnston, *The Illusion of Life*, 17.

64 Bob Thomas, "Disney Films Reflect Boss' Enthusiasm," *Des Moines Tribune*, September 7, 1953, 3.

65 Barry Linetsky, *The Business of Walt Disney and the Nine Principles of His Success* (Orlando: Theme Park Press, 2017), 70.

66 Barry Linetsky, *The Business of Walt Disney*, 72.

67 Don Peri, *Working with Walt: Interviews with Disney Artists* (Jackson: University Press of Mississippi, 2008), 124.

68 Don Peri, *Working with Walt*, 198.

69 Williams, *How to Be Like Walt*, 46.

70 Thomas, *The Walt Disney Biography*, 184.

71 Bob Thomas, "Disney's Interviews 'Different,'" *Oakland Tribune*, December 23, 1966, 13.

72 Wade Sampson, "The First Disney Television Christmas," MousePlanet.com, December 24, 2008, https://www.mouseplanet.com/8605/The_First_Disney_Television_Christmas.

73 Williams, *How to Be Like Walt*, 233.

74 Williams, *How to Be Like* Walt, 233.

75 Williams, *How to Be Like* Walt, 233.

76 Bob Thomas, "U.S. Kids Praised," Lansing (Michigan) *State Journal*, December 4, 1957, 20.

77 Jim Korkis, "And Now Your Host...Walt Disney," MousePlanet.com, May 25, 2016, https://www.mouseplanet.com/11422/And_Now_Your_Host_Walt_Disney.

78 Williams, *How to Be Like Walt*, 235.

79 Jim Korkis, "And Now Your Host...Walt Disney."

80 E. E. Edgar, "Famous Fables," Camden (New Jersey) *Courier-Post*, March 31, 1943, 14.

81 Peter Barks Kylling, "Carl Barks: The War Years," CBarks.dk, August 11, 2007, http://www.cbarks.dk/thewaryears.htm.

82 Wood Soanes, "Curtain Calls," *Oakland Tribune*, September 14, 1932, 24.

83 Soanes, "Curtain Calls," 24.

84 Michael Barrier, *The Animated Man: A Life of Walt Disney* (Berkeley: University of California Press, 2007), 173.

85 Rolly Crump, "Rolly Remembers Walt's Personal Touch," DisneyDispatch.com, March 28, 2011, http://www.disneydispatch.com/content/columns/the-truth-of-the-matter-is/2011/rolly-remembers-walts-personal-touch/.

86 Bob Gurr, remarks at "Walt Disney—Master of Dreamers: An Evening with Disney Legends Bob Gurr, Rolly Crump, and Friends," Highway 39 Event Center, Anaheim, California, October 13, 2018, transcribed by Peggy Matthews Rose.

87 Notes from a 2001 Disneyland cast member training class conducted by Ray Sidejas and Bruce Kimbrell.

88 Jim Korkis, *The Revised Vault of Walt: Unofficial Disney Stories Never Told* (Orlando: Theme Park Press, 2012), 64.

89 Craig Hodgkins, "Remembering Walt: A Labor of Love," CraigHodgkins.com, March 22, 2016, http://www.craighodgkins.com/2016/03/22/remembering-walt-a-labor-of-love/; David Koenig, "One of Walt's," MousePlanet.com, March 4, 2015, https://www.mouseplanet.com/10972/One_of_Walts.

90 Jim Korkis, *The Revised Vault of Walt*, 250.

91 Don Peri, *Working with Walt: Interviews with Disney Artists* (Jackson, MS: University Press of Mississippi, 2008), 170.

92 Craig Hodgkins, "Remembering Walt: A Labor of Love."

93 Freddy Martin, "The Bob Gurr Interview, Part 3: Walt & Bob & the Future," FreddyMartin.net, July 10, 2018, http://freddymartin.net/2018/07/10/bob-gurr-interview-part-3/.

94 Korkis, "And Now Your Host...Walt Disney."

95 Williams, *How to Be Like Walt*, 246.

96 Walter Ames, "Unknown Gets Disney Role in TV Film." *Los Angeles Times*, August 14, 1954, Part 2, 5.

97 Bob Thomas, "Hollywood," *Santa Cruz Sentinel*, February 21, 1955, 11; Fess Parker, "Our Kids are Hero-Hungry," *Los Angeles Times This Week* Magazine, October 9, 1955, 8–9.

98 Rolly Crump, "Rolly Crump's Jewish Small World Doll."

99 Julie Combs, Stacey Edmonson, and Sandra Harris, *The Trust Factor: Strategies for School Leaders* (New York: Routledge, 2013), 153.

100 Tony J. Tallarico, "The Grand Opening of Disneyland," ThisDayInDisneyHistory.com, http://thisdayindisneyhistory.homestead.com/disneylandgrandopening.html.

101 Leonard Mosley, *Disney's World: A Biography* (Lanham, MD: Scarborough House, 1990), 148–49.

102 Watts, *The Magic Kingdom*, 192.

103 Bill Peet, *Bill Peet: An Autobiography* (Boston: Houghton Mifflin, 1989), 171.

104 Hedda Hopper, "Disney Lives in World of Ageless Fantasy," *Los Angeles Times*, July 26, 1953, Part 4, 4.

105 Rolly Crump, "Rolly Remembers Walt's Personal Touch," DisneyDispatch.com, March 28, 2011, http://www.disneydispatch.com/content/columns/the-truth-of-the-matter-is/2011/rolly-remembers-walts-personal-touch/.

106 Todd Martens, "An Early Disneyland Designer Won Over Walt Disney with His Rebel Reputation," *Los Angeles Times*, September 7, 2018, https://www.latimes.com/entertainment/herocomplex/la-et-ms-rolly-crump-20180907-story.html.

107 Jeff James, "Leadership Lessons from Walt Disney—How to Inspire Your Team," Disney Institute Blog, March 21, 2018, https://www.disneyinstitute.com/blog/leadership-lessons-from-walt-disney—how-to/.

108 Gabler, *Walt Disney*, 240.

109 Florabel Muir, "Animated Cartoons Going Over Big," *New York Daily News*, December 1, 1929, 78.

110 Gabler, *Walt Disney*, 136.

111 Gabler, *Walt Disney*, 144.

112 Thomas, *Building a Company*, 262.

113 Willa Okker, "The Hollywood Parade," *San Mateo Times*, November 12, 1934, 6.

114 Bob Foster, "Screenings: Walt Will Be Sorely Missed," *San Mateo Times*, December 16, 1966, 27.

115 Author uncredited, "Orphans Attend Theater Party," *Los Angeles Times*, December 28, 1930, Part H, 2.

116 John G. West, *Walt Disney and Live Action: The Disney Studio's Live-Action Features of the 1950s and 60s* (Orlando: Theme Park Press, 2016), 30–31.

117 Bob Thomas, "Disney Had Patience When the Deficits Piled Up," *Oakland Tribune*, December 22, 1966, E21.

118 CalArts, "History: The CalArts Story," CalArts.edu, https://calarts.edu/about/institute/history.

119 John Hench with Peggy Van Pelt, *Designing Disney: Imagineering and the Art of the Show* (New York: Disney Editions, 2003), 22.

120 Barry Linetsky, *The Business of Walt Disney and the Nine Principles of His Success* (Orlando: Theme Park Press, 2017), 444–445.

121 West, *Walt Disney and Live Action*, vii.

122 Jim Korkis, *The Revised Vault of Walt*, 136.

123 Bob Thomas, "Prosperity Came to Walt Disney Studio Only Decade Ago; Had Faced Extinction," Gettysburg (Pennsylvania) *Times*, December 21, 1966, 13.

124 Thomas, "Prosperity Came," 13.

125 Thomas, "Prosperity Came," 13.

126 Jeff Rovin, ed., *Secrets from the World of Disney* (New York: American Media Specials, 2018), 18.

127 Hopper, "Disney Lives," 4.

128 Hopper, "Disney Lives," 4.

129 Charles Denton, "Dynamic Disney Works Long Days, Nights, Too," Lansing (Michigan) *State Journal*, February 19, 1957, 5.

130 Thomas, "Disney Had Patience," E21.

131 Pat Williams, *How to Be Like Walt: Capturing the Disney Magic Every Day of Your Life* (Deerfield Beach, FL: Health Communications, Inc., 2004), 374.

132 IMDb (Internet Movie Database), "Earl Felton Biography," IMDb.com, https://www.imdb.com/name/nm0271641/bio?ref_=nm_ov_bio_sm.

133 Mark I. Pinsky, *The Gospel According to Disney: Faith, Trust, and Pixie Dust* (Louisville, KY: Westminster John Knox Press, 2004), 18.

134 Pinsky, *Gospel According to Disney,* 18.

135 Ray Bradbury, Foreword to Howard E. Green and Amy Boothe Green's *Remembering Walt: Favorite Memories of Walt Disney* (New York: Disney Editions, 1999), vii.

136 Williams, *How to Be Like Walt*, 302.

137 Jim Korkis, "Walt's Smoking and Infamous Cough," MousePlanet.com, March 26, 2014, https://www.mouseplanet.com/10628/Walts_Smoking_and_Infamous_Cough.

138 Thomas Schatz, *Boom and Bust: American Cinema in the 1940s* (Berkeley: University of California Press, 1997), 165.

139 Gabler, *Walt Disney*, 455–56.

140 All quotes by Ms. Streep are from "Meryl Streep Slams Walt Disney, Celebrates Emma Thompson as a 'Rabid, Man-Eating Feminist,'" by Bennett Marcus, *Vanity Fair*, January 8, 2014, http://www.vanityfair.com/hollywood/2014/01/meryl-streep-emma-thompson-best-speech-ever.

141 Floyd Norman, "Sophie's Poor Choice," FloydNormanCom.Squarespace.com, January 8, 2014, http://floydnormancom.squarespace.com/blog/2014/1/8/sophies-poor-choice.

142 Gabler, *Walt Disney*, 124; Williams, *How to Be Like Walt*, 41.

143 David K. Williams, "Forgiveness: The Least Understood Leadership Trait in The Workplace," Forbes.com, January 5, 2015, https://www.forbes.com/sites/davidkwilliams/2015/01/05/forgiveness-the-least-understood-leadership-trait-in-the-workplace-2/

144 Dave Smith / Disney Book Group, *The Quotable Walt Disney* (New York: Disney Editions, 2001), 254.

145 Brian Hannan, *Coming Back to a Theater Near You: A History of Hollywood Reissues, 1914–2014* (Jefferson, NC: McFarland, 2016), 63.

146 Hannan, *Coming Back to a Theater*, 36.

147 Hopper, "Disney Lives," 4.

148 Geoff King, Claire Molloy, Yannis Tzioumakis, eds., *American Independent Cinema: Indie, Indiewood and Beyond* (New York: Routledge, 2013), 170.

149 Guinness World Records, "Highest-Grossing Animation at the Domestic Box Office (Inflation Adjusted)," GuinnessWorldRecords.com, http://www.guinnessworldrecords.com/world-records/highest-box-office-film-gross-for-an-animation-inflation-adjusted/.

150 Hopper, "Disney Lives."

151 David Oneal, "Extinct Attractions: Thurl Ravenscroft Documentary," online video, February 8, 2014, https://www.youtube.com/watch?time_continue=593&v=SjbnH9jNN1I.

152 Williams, *How to Be Like Walt*, 353.

153 Thomas, "Disney Had Patience," E21.

154 Thomas, "U.S. Kids Praised," 20.

155 Keith Gluck, "The Early Days of Audio-Animatronics," WaltDisney.org, June 18, 2013, https://www.waltdisney.org/blog/early-days-audio-animatronics.

156 Michael Broggie, *Walt Disney's Railroad Story: The Small-Scale Fascination that Led to a Full-Scale Kingdom* (Virginia Beach, VA: Donning, 1998), 186.

157 Gluck, "The Early Days of Audio-Animatronics."

158 Charles Denton, "Dynamic Disney Works Long Days," 5.

159 Charles Denton, "Story of Disney Tells Climb of Man with Ideas," Lansing (Michigan) *State Journal*, February 18, 1957, 1–2.

160 Michael Barrier, "Interviews: David Hand," MichaelBarrier.com, May 2003, http://www.michaelbarrier.com/Interviews/Hand/interview_david_hand.htm.

161 Frank Thomas and Ollie Johnston, *The Illusion of Life: Disney Animation* (New York: Hyperion, 1995), 25.

162 Walt Disney, "Growing Pains," *Journal of the Society of Motion Picture Editors*, January 1941, excerpted by Jim Korkis, "Walt Disney Remembers His Studio's 'Growing Pains,'" JimHillMedia.com, August 30, 2005, http://jimhillmedia.com/alumni1/b/wade_sampson/archive/2005/08/31/1276.aspx.

163 Rolly Crump, "Walt's Strawberry Waffles," DisneyDispatch.com, May 23, 2011, http://www.disneydispatch.com/content/columns/the-truth-of-the-matter-is/2011/walts-strawberry-waffles/.

164 Amy Boothe Green and Howard E. Green, *Remembering Walt: Favorite Memories of Walt Disney* (New York: Disney Editions, 1999), 66.

165 Jim Korkis, "Roy O. Disney Remembers His Kid Brother Walt," MousePlanet.com, November 30, 2016, https://www.mouseplanet.com/11616/Roy_O_Disney_Remembers_His_Kid_Brother_Walt.

166 Author uncredited, "The Pictures: The Cartoon and the Age," *London Observer*, March 9, 1930, 20.

167 Walt Disney, "Growing Pains."

168 John Crosby, "Ruinous Efficiency in Movie Making," *St. Louis Post-Dispatch*, February 9, 1949, 1D.

169 Jordan Zakarin, "Diane Disney Miller Remembers Dad: Walt's Secret Disneyland Apartment, His Passions & More," Huffington Post, February 7, 2012, https://www.huffpost.com/entry/walt-disneys-secret-disneyland-apartment-diane-disney-miller_n_1259421.

170 IMDb (Internet Movie Database), "Snow White and the Seven Dwarfs (1937) Trivia," IMDb.com, https://www.imdb.com/title/tt0029583/trivia.

171 Korkis, "Roy O. Disney Remembers."

172 Rudy Behlmer, *America's Favorite Movies: Behind the Scenes* (New York: Frederick Ungar Publishing, 1982), 60.

173 Staff writers, "Disney, 'Davy' Lead Yule Parade," *Long Beach Independent*, November 25, 1955, 5.

174   D23: The Official Disney Fan Club, "Mickey Mouse Club Circus at Disneyland," D23.com, November 25, 2009, https://d23.com/mickey-mouse-club-circus-to-open-here/.

175   Hopper, "Disney Lives," 4.

176   Jim Korkis, "Roy O. Disney Remembers."

177   Smith, *The Quotable Walt Disney*, 60.

178   Danton Walker, "Broadway," *New York Daily News*, January 11, 1954, 36.

179   John Lester, "Radio and Television," York (Pennsylvania) *Gazette and Daily*, March 19, 1954, 38.

180   Aline Mosby, United Press, "Around Hollywood," Medford (Oregon) *Mail Tribune,* May 11, 1954, 4.

181   D23, "Disneyland Construction Begins," D23 The Official Disney Fan Club, September 26, 2018, https://d23.com/this-day/disneyland-construction-begins/.

182   Mark Twain, *A Connecticut Yankee in King Arthur's Court* (London: Chatto & Windus, Piccadilly, 1889), 157.

183   Smith, *The Quotable Walt Disney*, 237.

184   Tom Nabbe, "Tom's in the Parade!," DisneyDispatch.com, March 29, 2011, http://disneydispatch.com/content/columns/the-adventures-of-tom-nabbe/2011/08-from-character-to-cast-member/; Tom Nabbe, "The Adventure of the Suspicious Secretary," DisneyDispatch.com, April 5, 2011, http://disneydispatch.com/content/columns/the-adventures-of-tom-nabbe/2011/06-the-adventure-of-the-suspicious-secretary/; Tom Nabbe, "The Adventure of Growing Up," DisneyDispatch.com, April 26, 2011, http://disneydispatch.com/content/columns/the-adventures-of-tom-nabbe/2011/07-the-adventure-of-growing-up/; Tom Nabbe, "From Character to Cast Member," DisneyDispatch.com, May 10, 2011, http://disneydispatch.com/content/columns/the-adventures-of-tom-nabbe/2011/08-from-character-to-cast-member/.

185   Note: In the article Rolly Crump wrote for DisneyDispatch.com, he referred to "Tampa Cloth;" we have used the correct term, "tapa cloth."

186   Rolly Crump, "The Tiki Room...Restaurant?," DisneyDispatch.com, April 18, 2011, http://www.disneydispatch.com/content/columns/the-truth-of-the-matter-is/2011/the-tiki-room-restaurant/; Rolly Crump, "Rolly Crump Pleases the Tiki Gods," DisneyDispatch.com, April 25, 2011, http://www.disneydispatch.com/content/columns/the-truth-of-the-matter-is/2011/rolly-crump-pleases-the-tiki-gods/; Rolly Crump, "Rolly Crump Learns How to Sculpt," DisneyDispatch.com, May 2, 2011, http://www.disneydispatch.com/content/columns/the-truth-of-the-matter-is/2011/rolly-crump-learns-how-to-sculpt/.

187   Rolly Crump, "Rolly Crump on Wheels."

188   Jim Korkis, "Walt in His Own Words," 5 Apr 2005, Jim Hill Media, http://jimhillmedia.com/alumni1/b/wade_sampson/archive/2005/04/06/1256.aspx; some instances of punctuation and capitalization have been changed by the authors for readability.

189   Smith, *The Quotable Walt Disney*, 123.

190   Disney, "The Marceline I Knew."

191   Jim Denney, "Walt's Mountains, Part 1: The Matterhorn," DizAvenue.com, August 20, 2017, https://www.dizavenue.com/2017/08/walts-mountains-part-i-matterhorn.html.

192   John Borden, "This Tiny Town is the Site of Disney's 'Lost' Park," CNN.com, June 12, 2018, https://www.cnn.com/travel/article/marceline-missouri-lost-disney-park/index.html; Jefferson, "Inside Walt Disney's Life in Marceline."

193   Jefferson, "Inside Walt Disney's Life in Marceline."

194   Staff writer, "Walt Disney Finds Evidence of Younger Days," *Kansas City Times*, July 5, 1956, 1.

195   Jefferson, "Inside Walt Disney's Life in Marceline."

196   Pinsky, *The Gospel According to Disney*, 21.

197   Boby Williams, post on Facebook.com, Disney History Institute page, September 1, 2017, https://www.facebook.com/groups/disneyhistoryinstitute/.

198   Rolly Crump, "The Small World Saga: Toys, Part 1," DisneyDispatch.com, May 30, 2011, http://www.disneydispatch.com/content/columns/the-truth-of-the-matter-is/2011/small-world-saga-toys-part-1/.

199 Rolly Crump, "The Small World Saga: Toys, Part 3," DisneyDispatch.com, June 13, 2011, http://www .disneydispatch.com/content/columns/the-truth-of-the-matter-is/2011/small-world-saga-toys-part-3/.

200 Rolly Crump, "The Small World Saga: Toys, Part 2," DisneyDispatch.com, June 6, 2011, http://www .disneydispatch.com/content/columns/the-truth-of-the-matter-is/2011/small-world-saga-toys-part-2/.

201 Smith, *The Quotable Walt Disney*, 177.

202 Lou Jobst, "Wisecracking, Winking HST Has Big Time at Disneyland," *Long Beach Independent Press-Telegram*, November 3, 1957, A1, A3.

203 L.A. Times Staff, "Eisenhowers, Family Guests at Disneyland," *Los Angeles Times*, December 27, 1961, 2; Associated Press, "Ike, Family in Visit to Disneyland," Indiana (Pennsylvania) *Gazette*, December 27, 1961, 46.

204 Paula Sigman Lowery, "Red, Walt, and Blue," Walt Disney Family Museum, July 4, 2011, https://www .waltdisney.org/blog/red-walt-and-blue.

205 Dave Mason, "The Story of Walt Disney's Final Official Visit to Disneyland," DizAvenue.com, October 7, 2016, https://www.dizavenue.com/2016/10/the-story-of-walt-disneys-final.html?m=1.

206 Hopper, "Disney Lives," 1.

207 Thomas, *Walt Disney*, 269–70.

208 Dave Mason, "Walt Disney's Final Public Appearance," DizAvenue.com, November 1, 2016, https:// www.dizavenue.com/2016/11/walt-disneys-final-public-appearance.html.

209 Jackson, ed., *Walt Disney: Conversations*, 137.

210 Linda Chion-Kenney, "A Kingdom of Believers," *Washington Post*, September 21, 1992, https://www .washingtonpost.com/archive/lifestyle/1992/09/21/a-kingdom-of-believers/198013be-0729-4bf9-a587 -b655d9b36007/?noredirect=on&utm_term=.d5a0d6fb6bb6.

211 Werner Weiss, "Disneyland One Year Old: A Press Release from July 18, 1956," Yesterland.com, July 15, 2016, https://www.yesterland.com/oneyear.html.

212 Dave DeCaro, "Nehru at Disneyland," DaveLandBlog.blogspot.com, December 2, 2012, https://dave landblog.blogspot.com/2012/12/nehru-at-disneyland.html.

213 Ray Bradbury, *Yestermorrow: Obvious Answers to Impossible Futures* (Santa Barbara: Joshua Odell Editions / Capra Press, 1991), 147.

214 Hopper, "Disney Lives," 1, 4.

215 Jim Korkis, "Walt Disney's Love of Trains: Part Two," MousePlanet.com, August 30, 2017, https://www .mouseplanet.com/11865/Walt_Disneys_Love_of_Trains_Part_Two.

216 Ibid.

217 Hopper, "Disney Lives."

218 Bob Thomas, *Walt Disney, Magician of the Movies* (New York: Grosset & Dunlap, 1966), 176.

219 Gluck, "Walt's Main Street—Part One: Inspirations."

220 Gabler, *Walt Disney*, 525.

221 Green and Green, *Remembering Walt*, 153.

222 Mike Vance and Diane Deacon, *Think Out of the Box* (Wayne, NJ: Career Press, 1995), 19–192.

223 Williams, *How to Be Like Walt*, 84.